Walden University

College of Social and Behavioral Sciences

This is to certify that the doctoral dissertation by

Michelle Tyrus

has been found to be complete and satisfactory in all respects,
and that any and all revisions required by
the review committee have been made.

Review Committee
Dr. Maria Van Tilburg, Committee Chairperson, Psychology Faculty
Dr. Scott Friedman, Committee Member, Psychology Faculty
Dr. Richard Thompson, University Reviewer, Psychology Faculty

Chief Academic Officer
Eric Riedel, Ph.D.

Walden University
2014

Abstract

Some studies have found that African-American men reared in single-parent households headed by a mother and with little or no paternal presence, may suffer from a variety of mental health problems as adults, which can be linked to higher rates of incarceration. This study's research problem set out to determine whether there was a connection between paternal presence, attachment style, and depression propensities among African-American men. The theoretical framework for this study was Bowlby's attachment theory. The purpose of this quantitative study was to examine whether an individual's attachment style mediates the relationship between depression propensity and paternal presence. Attachment styles were measured using the Measure of Attachment Qualities scale and depression symptoms were measured using the Beck Depression Inventory-II. Paternal presence was indicated by numbers of years the father was present in the home. The study participants included 92 African-American men between the ages of 18-55, who as a child resided in a single-parent home headed by a mother with little to no paternal presence. The participants were all recruited from a health fair held in Colorado. A 2x3 ANOVA was utilized to analyze the data. A small statistically significant interaction was found between attachment style, as 83 of the survey participants scored high in the avoidance range, and paternal presence and was determined to be linked with depression. Although not significant, the findings also suggest a relationship between the numbers of years a father was present in the home of African-American men and the development of depression later in life. As a result, the social change implication may be to develop community center parenting classes, which specifically addresses the importance of strong biological parental attachments during childhood.

The Relationship of Parental Presence and Family Structure on Attachment and

Depression Propensities for Adult African-American Men

by

Michelle Lorraine Tyrus

MA, University of Phoenix, 2005

BS, Kansas State University, 1996

Dissertation Submitted in Partial Fulfillment

of the Requirements for the Degree of

Doctor of Philosophy

Psychology

Walden University

2014

Dedication

This dissertation is dedicated to my brother, Michael Lawrence Tyrus. Although you left this world way too soon, you still remain my inspiration to pursue my dreams and you encourage me to be the best person that I can be. Thank you for being a great brother and friend – you will always be remembered.

I also dedicate this dissertation to my son, Michael Tyrus Hawkins. Thank you for being so patient with me while I fulfilled my dream of obtaining my doctorate degree. I hope that I will be an inspiration to you (and your soon to be little brother, Lawrence), as my brother was for me. Remember that you can do anything that you put your mind to.

Acknowledgments

I have been very fortunate to have so many wonderful people enter my life and encourage and help me to achieve this goal. I would like to first thank Dr. Reginald Taylor, who believed in me so much that he was willing to be my preliminary chairperson even before I was ready for the dissertation class. Thank you so much, Dr. Taylor, for believing in me and hanging in there with me through this long process. I would also like to thank Dr. Scott Friedman, who agreed to be a committee member despite an extremely busy schedule; Dr. Richard Thompson from my URR committee; and Dr. Maria van Tilburg. I thank you for your thoroughness and belief in me. I also cannot forget to thank Dr. John Nicoletti, my practicum and intern supervisor and a man whom I consider to be a great mentor and friend. Thank you for all your encouraging words and guidance throughout the years. You took a chance on me and believed in me, for that I will always be grateful!

To all the men that volunteered to participate in my study: thank you for your support, without which this would not be possible. My many friends and family who put up with me throughout this process and always encouraged me when I felt that I would never finish need to be acknowledged and thanked. I want to especially acknowledge my mother and my friend Sharon Holmes. Mom, you always knew that I would finish. Thank you for listening to me and allowing me to vent when I needed to. Sharon, you are so much more than a friend…you are like a sister to me. I want to thank you for always being my support when I had no one else. You are a wonderful friend and I am honored to have you in my life.

I am truly humbled by all of you and sincerely thank you.

Table of Contents

List of Tables

List of Figures

Chapter 1: Introduction

Since the early 1990s, a large and growing proportion of children have been raised in nontraditional family homes. This increase has been related to the rise in divorce, children born out of wedlock, and co-parenting (unmarried) family structures (Blau & Wilbert van der Klaauw, 2008). Consequently, this increase in nontraditional family homes has resulted in many children living in single-parent homes headed by a mother with limited or no biological paternal parent present. A longitudinal study conducted of 12- to 16-year-olds in 1997 by United States Department of Labor Bureau discovered that 74% of the non-Hispanic, Caucasian children lived with both biological parents, but only 33% of the African-American children did so. Moreover, they reported that 49% of African-American mothers never lived with their child's biological father. This study is important, because it brings awareness of the disparity in the homes of African-American children and non-Hispanic, Caucasian children; however, it does not explore the long-term impact being raised without a biological father in the home can have on African-American children.

Several studies have explored how paternal absence impacts incarceration rates and drug use among African-American men (Mandara, Rogers, & Zinbarg, 2011; Wileman & Western, 2010). However, few studies have examined whether limited or no biological paternal presence during childhood may be related to attachment difficulties and depression in adulthood among African-American man.

In effort to test this hypothesis, I investigated whether there was an association between attachment style and the development of depressive symptoms among African-

American men raised in single, mother-headed households. Lastly, I examined whether there was a high propensity for depression in adulthood for African-American men who were raised with limited or no biological paternal presence in single-parent, mother-headed homes during childhood. In effort to better understand how this type of environment would have a negative impact on an individual, it is necessary to delve into the study's background.

Background

It is believed by many that negative life events during childhood, such as the absence of an attachment figure, may cause a child to suffer from learned helplessness, which may later develop into depression (Ainsworth, 2000; Alloy, Abramson, Grant, & Liu, 2009; Baldaro, 2010; Beck, 1967; Bowlby, 1980; Cole et al., 2007; Iacoviello, Alloy, Abramson, & Choi, 2010; Prior & Glasser, 2006; Surcinelli, Rossi, Montebarocci, 2010). Cole et al. (2007) set out to test this hypothesis. They gave kindergarten-age children a set of unsolvable puzzles followed by a set of solvable puzzles. During the trials the researchers noted that the children began to view the puzzles as hopeless and increasingly became unmotivated and would refuse to participate. This behavior continued even when the puzzles were solvable. The researchers gleaned from these trials and through parents' reports that some of the children had been exposed to negative life events and/or adverse parenting styles, which contributed to the development of the learned helplessness observed in the trials (Cole et al., 2007). This study was important, as it demonstrated that negative life events and adverse parenting during childhood may contribute to the development of depression.

There are a number of scholars who agreed with Cole et al. (2007), as they theorized that negative attachment experiences in childhood increase the risk for developing depression later in life (Ainsworth, 2000; Alloy, Abramson, Grant, & Liu, 2009; Baldaro, 2010; Beck, 1967; Bowlby, 1980; Cole et al., 2007; Iacoviello, Alloy, Abramson, & Choi, 2010; Prior & Glasser, 2006; Surcinelli, Rossi, Montebarocci, 2010). Cicchetti, Toth, and Lyncy (1995) hypothesized that negative attachments during childhood may create insecurely attached people and that these individuals are more susceptible to develop learned helplessness and consequently have fewer coping methods available to handle stress. Cicchetti et al. (1995) explained that individuals become preconditioned to develop a negative self-schema of being unlovable or undesirable, attributing this development to helplessness and a lack of felt security.

This led Cole et al. (2007) to conclude that there was a direct link between learned helplessness and depression. They hypothesized that environmental factors were the precursor to their development, as they discussed that negative environmental factors such as traumatic or negative life events (any situations that the child feels that they have no control) and/or problematic parental care (lack of support, harsh parenting, and unsympathetic feedback) all encouraged the development of learned helplessness. The authors further added that the development of learned helplessness during childhood hinders a child's ability to develop positive self-esteem and confidence. Consequently, when the child grows older his self-view of incompetence would become the natural precursor to the development of depression. They further hypothesized that when the child enters into adolescence and he develops a more complex thought system, he would also carry with him a more complex depressive pattern of thinking that may continue with him into adulthood.

Alloy et al. (2009) expounded on this subject with a study that set out to determine whether negative thought processes would lead to the development of hopelessness and later develop into depression. The researchers' findings suggests that individuals who possess a depressogenic thought process were more likely to engage into a negative cognitive style during times of stressful life events, and they had a predisposition to perceive these negative life events as constant rather than fleeting.

The research conducted by Alloy et al. (2009) concurred with the earlier findings by Bowlby (1963). Bowlby's writings explained that depression has a direct relation to childhood experiences and is also correlated with the circumstance and severity of those experiences. He further added that positive relationships with attachment figures during childhood are associated with one's ability to establish a positive self-image. Accordingly, if an individual experienced weak childhood attachments he/she is likely to develop a negative self-image and feel unsupported, lonely, sad, and unlovable. Compared to someone who had strong ties during childhood, they are more prone to suffer from depression. Consequently, the aforementioned scholars have all concluded that there is a correlation between weak attachment to one's parental figures during childhood and depression.

Problem Statement

In my investigation of this topic, I failed to find research that examined the interrelationship between attachment to a paternal figure, attachment style, and depression symptoms. Several studies focused on the development of behavioral problems and depression in later life due to negative childhood experiences, such as harsh parenting and traumatic life events (Cole et al., 2007; Haine, Ayers, Sandler, Wolchik & Weyer, 2003; Kliewer & Sandler, 1992). Accordingly, children who are raised in single-parent households are at risk to develop depression. The current study is necessary and important because African-American children are more likely than Caucasian and Hispanic children to live in mother-headed, single-parent homes. Additionally, African-American men who are raised without their biological father in a single mother-headed home have an increase risk to develop depression. This gap in the literature was addressed by designing a study focused on the interrelationship between limited or no biological paternal figure in the home, attachment levels (secure and avoidant) and depression symptoms among African-American men between the ages of 18 to 55 years.

Purpose of the Study

The purpose of this quantitative, retrospective, study was to examine the interrelationship between African-American men paternal attachment and depression propensities. Moreover, this research examined whether this relationship was mediated by years of paternal presence (limited or no presence). The first independent variable, paternal attachment, was defined as the desire to be in close proximity or in contact with one's paternal figure particularly in times of fear (Bowlby, 1982). Paternal attachment had four levels: secure, avoidant, ambivalent (worry) and ambivalent (merger). The second independent variable was the years of paternal presence in the household. Paternal presence in the household had three levels: (a) less than one year, (b) one to six years, and (c) seven to twelve years. The dependent variable was depression symptoms that were characterized by "low mood, pessimism, self-criticism, and retardation or agitation" (Beck, 1967, p. 10).

Research Questions and Hypotheses

Research Questions

1. Is there an association between attachment and depression, in African-American men between the ages of 18 to 55 years?

2. Is there an association between parental presence and depression in African-American men between the ages of 18 to 55 years?

3. Is the effect of paternal presence on depression different for secure versus avoidant attachment?

Hypotheses

1. Null Hypothesis (H_0): There will be no significant main effect of paternal attachment on depression.

   Alternative Hypothesis (H_1): There will be a significant main effect of paternal attachment on depression.

2. Null Hypothesis (H_0): There will be no significant main effect of parental presence on depression.

   Alternative Hypothesis (H_1): There will be a significant main effect of parental presence on depression.

3. Null Hypothesis (H_0): There will be no attachment by paternal presence interaction effect on depression.

Alternative Hypothesis (*H*1): There will be an attachment by paternal presence interaction on depression.

Theoretical Framework

The attachment theory system developed by Bowlby (1969) provided the theoretical basis for this study. Attachment theory has been utilized to explain how positive or negative experiences with one's caregivers during childhood will form a *working model* from which future relations with others will be viewed. This working model includes expectation about whether a loved one will be available for support in times of need. A working model stays constant through one's lifespan and is essential in determining how one view's oneself and others (Berry, Barrowclough & Wearden, 2009).

As applied to this study, attachment theory holds that I would expect my independent variables, levels of attachment (secure, avoidant, ambivalent worry, and ambivalent merger) and paternal presence to be associated with the dependent variable, depression. This is theorized because researchers have proposed that individuals, who were reared in a single-parent home without both attachment figures are more likely to develop insecure attachments which increases the risk of depression (Newland & Cole, 2010). A more detailed examination of attachment literature will be provided in chapter 2.

Nature of the Study

I chose a quantitative, retrospective, survey design for this study. This design was chosen to examine my research questions. I did not manipulate any variables. The participants were African-American men between 18-and 55 years of age residing in

Colorado. African-American men were chosen for this study, because there are high percentages that were raised in single-parent, mother headed households, who are incarcerated. I wanted to determine whether there was a correlation with the loss of a biological father and the development of depression later in life. Moreover, the ages chosen for the study provided a broad range in adulthood to ascertain whether there were long-term consequences from being reared in a home without a biological father.

Definitions of Terms

Anhedonia: The loss of interest in activities and behaviors that one used to find pleasurable (Chrisler & McCreary, 2010).

Anxious-resistant attachment: An attachment style that was presented in the attachment theory by Bowlby (1963). People who display this attachment style have difficulty of trusting strangers and express distress symptoms when not in proximity to their attachment figures (Ainsworth, Blehar, Walls, & Waters, 1978; Bowlby, 1973; Peluso, Peluso, White & Kern, 2004).

Attachments: Relational connections established with others (Nelson & Bennett, 2008).

Attachment styles: Patterns of behavior established by Bowlby (1973) in his attachment theory. These are various attachment styles, which indicate the type of expectations one has about the behaviors of loved ones (Prior, Glaser, & Kingsley, 2006). These include anxious attachment, avoidant attachment, and secure attachment.

Avoidant attachment: A type of attachment pattern defined in the attachment theory was coined by Bowlby (1973). This type of attachment style is identified by an avoidance of the formation of relationships and the refusal to allow others to form relationships with them (Prior, Glaser, & Kingsley, 2006).

African-American: Defined in this study as individuals who identify themselves as of predominantly African-American heritage.

Behavioral system: This serves as the premise for the attachment theory developed by Bowlby's (1963). Humans were born with instinctive behaviors that allow one to remain in close proximity with an attachment figure. A common example of this behavior is crying (Prior, Glaser, & Kingsley, 2006).

Berkeley Adult Attachment Interview (AAI): An assessment tool that measures adult attachment behaviors and patterns (Main, 1996).

Depression: In the context of this paper, depression refers to a low mood in which there is an aversion to many activities that are normally enjoyed or carried out. It will also affect the individual's physical well-being, behavior, thoughts, and general emotional state. In this study depression was measured with the Beck Depression Inventory. The instrument takes a two factor approach to depression assuming that it will involve both somatic and affective components (Beck, 2009). It therefore includes measures of cognitive items such as feelings of being punished and guilt, as well as measurements for physical symptoms such as lack of interest in sex, weight loss, and fatigue. The latest version of this instrument, the BDI-II was developed in 1996.

Single mother headed household: This is operationally defined as a household in which the father is present less than 33% of the time and contributes less than 33% of the household income (FIFCFS, 2012).

Strange Situation Study: An investigative model developed by Ainsworth (1978) to determine attachment relationships between biological mothers and their infants by observing child reactions to short separations from the mother (Ainsworth, Blehar, Walters & Walls, 1978).

Assumptions

Major assumptions of this study was that the validity and reliability of the Measure of Attachment Qualities and the Beck Depression Inventory were sound and appropriate tools to measure attachment styles and depression symptoms of the participants in the study. Additionally, I assumed that the participants would respond in a forthcoming and honest manner to the items on the depression scale, demographic survey, and the attachment tool. Furthermore, an assumption was made about the intellectual and cognitive abilities of the participants, as I assumed that these abilities were of an adequate level to assist the participants in comprehending the questions that were presented on the depression scale and the attachment measure. Finally, another assumption that I made was that the participants would be able to fully comprehend the meaning of paternal presence, which was the number of years the father was present in the childhood home.

Delimitations of the Study

This study has a number of delimitations. The first delimitation has to do with the study only being done in the United States. This study may not have applicability in other nations. The United States is unique in many ways. It is a capitalist mixed economy with the advantage of many natural resources and an infrastructure that is well developed. The country also has high productivity levels (Wright & Czelusta, 2007).

The scope of the study was also limited to single-mother headed households. Consequently, this delimitation omitted alternative family units – an increasingly important household segment. For example, there are a growing number of single father headed households as well. It would be interesting to compare this group to that of the single-mother headed household as well as the traditional household with a mother and father present. There are also a large number of nontraditional families that are now becoming more common. For example, there are now some same-sex unions that either retain the children from a former relationship or adopt. This means there are families that have two fathers or two mothers. The results of this study do not yield information on these types of families, even if they reside in the United States.

An additional delimitation was that the operational definitions being used in this study was limited by the accuracy of the instruments employed (Marczyk, DeMatteo & Festinger, 2005). For example, the Beck Depression inventory is a well-accepted instrument (Beck & Alford, 2009), but it suffers from the same limitations as any self-report inventory: scores can be minimized or exaggerated according to the person who is completing the questionnaire. Also, the way in which the instrument is administered can affect the final score obtained. If the individual completing the questionnaire is filling out the form when other people are present it may significantly influence their responses. There was also the possibility that subtle social expectations could be communicated inadvertently by researchers administering the instrument. Many of these delimitations also apply to the other instruments that were being used for this study (Marczyk et al., 2005).

Limitations of the Study

I did not examine whether being raised with a single mother as head of the household created an economic disadvantage that caused depression. Likewise, I did not include in the sample men who were raised in a home with a male figure other than the biological father present. The sample was also limited to men between the ages of 18 to 55 years of age. I did not examine whether a mother's personality traits or attachment to the mother could be associated with feelings of helplessness on the part of the male child that in turn might cause a male child to suffer from depression. Also, I did not include in my study single parent homes headed by mothers who have successfully raised African-American males, who do not suffer from attachment disorders. Finally, because this study's measurements were based on participants' self-reports, I did not examine whether the participants may not always be truthful or may have forgotten depression symptoms.

Significance of the Study

A literature review did not yield any studies in peer-reviewed journals that used attachment patterns to examine the impact of single mother-headed households on depression in adult African-American men. There are a considerable number of articles (described in Chapter 2) that explored the relationship between childhood attachment patterns and depression. There are also a number of studies that investigated adult attachment patterns and depression. It was previously discussed in this chapter how there have been investigations on the application of attachment theories to adult relationships.

There is also a considerable amount of literature on the negative effect of father absence on African-American men. However, the majority of these studies focused on anger and issues related to criminality. Limited research was found that focused on attachment and depression in relation to African-American men who were raised in a mother headed single-parent home. This research would be beneficial, because it could assist in spreading community awareness.

Because of the rising number of African-American men in prison, many communities have established youth mentor programs in order to provide African-American men with stable, male, role models. These programs have been formed around the hypothesis that a high number of African-American men are being raised in urban environments in a single-parent home, without their biological father; consequently, they are more susceptible to commit criminal acts; therefore, they are more likely to be imprisoned than Caucasian men (Battle, 2002; Daniels, 1986; Wildeman, 2009). However, most of these programs fail to recognize that many of the African-American men who are raised in these single-parent, mother-headed homes may also suffer from depression and thus require therapeutic initiatives that focus on understanding and alleviating depression symptoms.

The number of single-parent homes headed by a mother has risen since the early 1990s and researchers have found that men who are raised in a single-parent home headed by a mother are more likely to suffer from mental health problems that may extend into adulthood, such as low self-esteem, abandonment issues, and attachment difficulties (Caldera, 2004; Department of Labor Statistics Bureau of Labor, 2013; Liu,

2007). Moreover, research has found that many African-American men raised in these environments often suffer from depression that often goes unrecognized and never treated (Allen, Hauser, & Borman-Spurrell, 1996; Armsden, McCauley, Greenberg, Burke, Mitchell, 1990; Brumariu & Kerns, 2010; Kogan & Brody; Oliver, 2003; Rohde, Lewinsohn, & Sedey, 1990). This study may help shed light on a pervasive syndrome that is often unrecognized and untreated and may encourage changes in mentor programs to reduce this problem. It is important to emphasize that there are many examples of single-parent homes headed by mothers who have successfully raised children. Single-mothers can and do raise children who are well adjusted and do not have increased risk for attachment disorders and depression. Having at least one secure attachment figure is important in a child's life, when fathers are absent as caregivers, mothers have to take on more responsibility. If the mother has issues that prevent her from being a consistent provider, and there is no father to fill the gap, providing training to single-mothers may also help in negating the absence of a father in the household.

Summary

A significant number of studies have, examined the general impact of being raised in single mother households on adult African-American men. Most of these studies focused on development of depression in later life due to negative childhood experiences, such as harsh parenting and traumatic life events or economic stressors that could contribute to adult depression. Additionally, other studies focused attention on depression caused by the lack of a father in the home. This study contributes to the literature by exploring the risk of insecure attachment and depression in adult African-American men raised in single mother headed households without a biological paternal figure.

Four additional chapters complete this dissertation. Chapter 2 is a literature review that focuses on attachment theory research, with a special emphasis on early childhood attachment problems and the development of depression in adulthood. Chapter 3 consists of a detailed outline of the research design and methodology. This chapter will also include a thorough description of the setting, sample, sampling method, sample size, and eligibility criteria for participants in the study. There will be an explanation of the materials and instruments used as well as a detailed description of the data. The data analysis process will be described in this section.

Chapter 4 will explore the study's results. Research questions and hypotheses will be tested. Additionally, the reliability of the utilized attachment and depression will be discussed. These findings will be interpreted in chapter 5. This chapter will include a conclusion of the research and reference the outcomes that were established in chapter 4. Also, a discussion of the study's limitations will be presented. Implications for social change and recommendations for actions will be given here as well.

Chapter 2: Literature Review

The theoretical framework for this study was derived from John Bowlby's (1969)

attachment theory and Aaron Becks' (1967) cognitive theoretical perspective of

depression. The purpose of this quantitative research was to determine whether or not

adult African-American men reared in single-mother headed households have an

increased propensity for attachment and depression difficulties. The working hypothesis

used was that the lack of a primary attachment figure (e.g., a biological paternal figure)

causes African-American men to suffer attachment and depression difficulties in

adulthood. I specifically set out to investigate attachment and depression propensities in

African-American men who had been reared in single-parent households headed by

mothers without their biological fathers.

Organization of the Chapter

This chapter's objective is to provide a critical examination of peer-reviewed

research that explores the dynamics of separation or loss of a father during childhood and

the potential consequences that a child may suffer in adulthood. There will be a review of

the collection of works on childhood attachment. Followed by an exploration of studies

that investigates adult attachments, including emotion consequences, and a review of

developing attachment measures. Because depression has been frequently associated with

attachment, the second section will include a discussion of the theoretical perspectives on

depression within the context of attachment. This section will present an analysis of

cognitive schemas that are theorized to be associated with depression and attachment issues. Thirdly, a discussion of risk factors that are related to African-American men who were raised without a biological fathers in single parent, mother-headed homes will also be explored. In particular, this chapter will align the theories of attachment and depression in relation to African-American men. Finally, the fourth section will include a discussion of research questions along with a summary of related research..

Description of Literature Search

The literature search initially focused on books that provided the foundational theories of attachment and depression symptoms. These works are important to the study because they were developed by the founders of these theories. After this preliminary search was completed, the National Institute of Mental Health (NIMH) and Federal Interagency Forum on Child and Family Statistics websites were used to obtain statistics about the number of African-American sons growing up without a father and information on depression in African-American men. Furthermore, electronic databases (PsycARTICLES, PsycBOOKS, PsycINFO, PsycLIT, Psychiatry Online, Questia online, SocINDEX) were searched for the following terms: *Men and insecure attachments, African-American men, Black men, attachment, single-parent homes, depression, fathers and sons, cognitive schemas, insecure attachments, absentee fathers, adult men, adult children, and adult depression*. This search began on January 2009 and continued until an exhaustive search was completed on August 2013. In order to be included in this search, the studies had to consist of the following components: adult depression, attachment disorder, African-American men in single-parent homes, attachment, paternal figure, cognitive schemas, absent father and depression.

Bowlby Attachment Theory

Many theorists posited that negative early childhood attachment experiences are most notably linked with the development of depression (Ainsworth, 2000; Bowlby, 1980; Prior & Glasser, 2006; Surcinelli, Rossi, Montebarocci, Baldaro, 2010). Bowlby (1980) associated this connection to the significant role that early experiences with caregivers play in the formation of healthy views of themselves and the world around them. This research serves as the foundation on which the current study is based.

John Bowlby (1907-1990) was known for introducing the world to the importance of attachment during childhood. He believed that early bonds –established in infancy- influence relationships in adulthood. If an infant can depend on his/her caregiver it will develop a 'working model' of relationships that is characterized by a belief that it can trust loved ones. If the infant on the other hand, cannot consistently be certain the caregiver will respond to his/her needs, the child will develop a 'working model' of relationships that is characterized by insecurity and mistrust (Bowlby, 1973). His works were concentrated around developing an understanding of the tandem workings of the environment and learned behavioral output. Bowlby's theory brought attention to a group of behaviors intended to maintain proximity to the caregiver in order to feel protected and secure (Cassidy, 1999).

Attachment behavior is "the result of the activity of behavioral systems that have a continuing set-goal, the specification of which is a certain sort of relationship to another specified individual" (Bowlby, 1982, p. 271). As said before, these behavioral systems or working models provide the stage for the later development of attachment in adulthood

(Bowlby, 1982). Attachment is an instinctive behavior pattern that necessitates adults to care for their children and makes children seek out their parents for protection and security (Bowlby, 1973; Prior, Glaser, & Kingsley, 2006). This need is essential during infancy and childhood when the child is growing and vulnerable to its environment. Later in this review, there will be an examination of different instances where this necessary attachment did not occur.

Attachment theory was illuminated by the study of animal behavior, as human attachment behavior was believed by Bowlby to be a consequence of an evolutionary instinct to preserve human kind that was reminiscent of animal species' life cycles (Bowlby, 1973). The basic tenet of Bowlby's theory centers on the instinctual need for survival and protection. As he explained, in order for early humans to avoid extinction, the first humans learned that it was necessary to live together in groups to effectively stave off predators, breed, hunt, and gather food (Bowlby, 1973). It was theorized by Bowlby (1973), when humans evolved, their protection mechanism remained stagnate and was responsible for an infant's instinctual need to remain in proximity of their caregivers. According to attachment theory, when children are fearful and distressed they desire to be in proximity to their caregiver in order to be protected from harm. This instinctual need prompts the infant to cry, reach, suck, and cling for survival purposes (Bowlby, 1973). In compliment to the child's proximity-seeking attachment behavior, the attachment figure is designed with an instinctual need to respond to the attachment behavior exhibited by the child. The caregiver's responses to the child's needs play a large role on the child's developing view of himself and others (Brown, 2007). Bowlby's attachment theory introduced evolutionary benefits of attachment behavior to the forefront (Bowlby, 1969), in particular behaviors that were aligned with different forms of attachment classification (Ainsworth, 1973; Hesse, 1999), and threats linked to psychopathology which are associated with various patterns of behavior and self-worth (Cummings & Cicchetti, 1990). These attachment behaviors are obtained from one's environment and held within the internal working model (IWM) and will be discussed in the next section (Bowlby, 1980).

Internal working model. An essential component of the attachment theory is the internal working model, as Bowlby believed that dysfunctional interpersonal attachments throughout one's life cycle effect the development of the internal working model (Bowlby, 1980). Internal working models are representational models that assist us in conceptualizing the self, others, and attachment situations in connection with the world, through these models strategies and coping skills are developed in order to achieve purposeful goals (Bowlby, 1980; Griffith, 2004; Mercer, 2006). The literature reveals that the internal working model is the key controller of attachment behavior, as it is responsible for governing one's expectations and cognitive representations linked with essential intimate relationships (Griffith, 2004). A child formulates internal working models for each attachment figure on the basis of the experiences they have with each caregiver; hence attachment behavior is believed to be elicited by one's environment (Bowlby, 1980; Griffith, 2004; Prior, Glaser, & Kingsley, 2006). Information is gathered from the environment and then analyzed in terms of the significance to the individual and their attachments; a plan of action is then developed and executed (Bowlby, 1980). The internal working model serves as a self-monitoring device that guides one's expectations

of how others would treat them (Bowlby, 1973). A working model consists of two parts:

the environmental model, which is depended upon the compilation of one's experience,

and an organismic model that relies on the individual's skills and abilities. In order for

both working models to be useful, the models have to be kept up-to-date (Bowlby, 1980).

New experiences can integrate into the working models; however, this information is

shaped by the original model (Bowlby, 1982; Prior, Glasser, & Kinglsey, 2006).

Bowlby (1982) hypothesized the following: A number of measures are required if

an organism is to exploit a working model. First, the model must be built in accordance

with available data. Secondly, if the model is to be of use in novel situations, it must be

extended imaginatively to cover potential realities as well as experienced ones. Thirdly,

any model, whether applicable to an experienced world or to a potential one, must be

tested for internal consistency (or, in technical language, for compliance with the axioms

of the theory of sets). The more adequate the model the more accurate its predictions; and

the more comprehensive the model the greater the number of situations in which its

predictions apply.

The attachment literature revealed that a supportive parent-child relationship is an

essential component in the formation of a child's positive worldview (Bretherton, 1990).

It is posed that individuals who are raised by attentive, responsive, and caring parents

develop healthy internal working models that allow them feelings of security and

confidence (Grossmann, Grossmann, & Waters, 2005; Griffith, 2004; Kenny & Sirin,

2006). Because these individuals are able to draw upon positive environmental experiences with attachment figures, they are easily able to trust new attachment figures that enter into their environment. Likewise, children with a positive internal working model are easily able to cope with stressful situations, as they are confident in themselves and others (Kenny & Sirin, 2006). On the contrary, children who have experienced traumatic events (such as illness, death of a family member, change in living arrangements, and excessive social stressors) or repetitive experience with attachment figures, who are unavailable or detached, internalize and integrate this negative experience into their working model. When they enter into adulthood and engage with other attachment figures, they draw upon this past information (Bowlby, 1982; Del Guidice, 2009; Sherry, Lyddon, & Henson, 2007).

Bretherton (1990) elaborated that the internal working model is an interdependent hierarchy composition of one's self, world, and others that acts jointly and reciprocally onto one another. Consequently, people who have unhealthy or undeveloped internal working models often have self-defeating views of themselves and the world. These individuals tend to focus solely on new information that corroborates their existing beliefs and selectively ignore contradictory new information. As a result, people with unhealthy internal working models often suffer from depression (Griffith, 2004). The development of abnormal internal working models will be discussed next.

Attachment relational stages. After a child develops an attachment relationship to his caregiver and the caregiver unexpectedly departs, the child will behave in a predictable and sequential fashion (Bowlby, 1973). First, separation of the attachment figure from the infant will encourage the child to enter into the *protest* stage. During this stage he experiences separation anxiety, in which he feels unrealistic and repetitive anxiety after separation or potential separation of an attachment figure (Eisen & Schaefer, 2005). Often the child will express his displeasure by protesting forcibly and desperately attempting to locate the mother or caregiver. Next, the child will enter into the *despair* stage, which is akin to feelings of grief and mourning (Bowlby, 1980). During this stage the child's attention remains focused on the whereabouts of the caregiver and continues to attempt to locate them and despairs the fact that he is unable to locate him or her (Bowlby, 1980). A prolonged separation from the caregiver may cause a child in this stage to develop learned helplessness. The child's inability to resolve the desire to be in proximity to the caregiver leaves the child with a feeling of helplessness that remains with him even when faced with a problem that he can fix. Consequently, this state of mind leads the child into a depressive disorder (Bowlby, 1980; Seligman, 1975).

The last stage the child enters into is the *detachment* stage where he sets up a defense. He no longer looks for the caregiver and becomes emotionally detached from them. If the period of attachment is not too long, the child will re-acclimate back to the caregiver. However, the child will insist on staying in proximity to the caregiver for several days and sometimes weeks and will experience slight anxiety if he believes that he will lose the attachment figure again. These phases of separation are all inclusive, as one could not exist without the other (Bowlby, 1980).

Most children do not experience prolonged separation from their caregivers and form secure attachments with them. Those children who are not able to form secure attachments, showed a variety of behaviors that can be divided in three general classes of insecure attachment: insecure-resistant, anxious ambivalent, and disorganized (see Table 1 for review of attachment classifications). Children who are classified in the *insecure-resistant/anxious-ambivalent* group are often plagued with abnormal anxieties centering on their self-worth and the potentiality for others to love them and protect them in times of perceived danger (Howe, Brandon, Hinings, & Schofield, 1999). They are regularly viewed by others as dismissive, socially reserved, and having little affect. As adults these children often lessen the importance of attachment relationships, as they view others as unavailable and possibly rejecting. Likewise, they experience extreme anxiety when entering into close relationships; therefore, they are known to engage in social defense mechanistic behaviors, which might include withholding their emotions, withdrawing, and displaying a lack of emotional empathy towards others (Howe, Brandon, Hinings, & Schofield, 1999). During difficult times, they may view others as dismissive and emotionally unavailable. Because they are less likely to seek help from others, they are more susceptible to suffer from a psychological illness, such as depression, if untreated could possibly develop into a physical illness (Howe, Brandon, Hinings, & Schofield, 1999).

Anxious-avoidant attachment is also included in the insecure attachment group and occurs when the individual exudes a lack of confidence and expects rejection from others. This individual's needs have not been met as a child and may have felt rejected by his attachment figure; consequently, he learns to actively avoid his caregivers in times of stress. This avoidance becomes a safety measure, as it allows him to avoid further rejection (Howe, Brandon, Hinings, & Schofield, 1999).

An additional attachment classification has been recently identified as *disorganized attachment* (Howe, Brandon, Hinings, & Schofield, 1999). This new attachment behavior is a combination of anxious-avoidant and anxious-ambivalent, because of its complex makeup it is not easily identified (Howe, Brandon, Hinings, & Schofield, 1999). *Disorganized attachment* is often seen in children who have suffered losses and were unable to resolve them or in children who have been severely traumatized. All four attachment classifications are relevant to Bowlby's (1980) theory that children will seek out and form some type of attachment, regardless of the environment the child is exposed to, in reciprocation to the response of the caregiver.

It should be noted that Bowlby developed many of his theories well over 30 years ago. Since that time there have been concerns that his attachment theory only applies to infants and cannot be extrapolated to adults (Horowitz & Strack, 2011). A number of researchers have found that adult attachment styles often center on anxiety and avoidance. The avoidance indicates how much a person trusts others to have general intentions of goodwill. Their level of anxiety regarding relationships represents their belief regarding the future availability and reliability of a partner. These factors can be understood as being qualitatively different than those presented by Bowlby (Horowitz & Strack, 2011).

However, similar attachment behaviors can be observed in children and adults. For example, during infancy secure infants primarily explored the world without hesitation, only periodically taking note of the caregiver's whereabouts and all the while maintaining an even balance between contact with attachment figure and attention to the environment (Main, 1996). Likewise, during adulthood, securely attached adults sustain an even balance between self-autonomy and having close and intimate relationships with romantic attachments (Feeney, Noller, & Hanraham, 1994). Secure adults typically displayed more confidence in their abilities and themselves and were less likely to avoid close relationships (Feeney et al., 1994; Ross, McKim, & Ditommaso, 2006). Another example is of infants who are insecure-avoidantly attached. They rarely cried upon separation from attachment figures, nor did they exhibit anger or emotion. Similarly, in adulthood, insecure-avoidant attachment is associated with giving less importance to intimate relationships and the need for others (Main, 1996; Feeney et al., 1994). If these adults discuss their experience as a child, they often relay that they had a positive relationship with their parents; however, they rarely are able to substantiate these claims (Main, 1996). Another infantile example of insecure-ambivalent behavior, is the inability to form consistent strategies to achieve comfort from the attachment figure in times of stress. Infants classified in this category were observed to focus most of their attention and awareness on the attachment figure rather than their environment, which suggests that these children spend less time exploring their environment due to the fact that they are overly focused on maintaining proximity to their attachment figure (Main, 1996). Likewise, during adulthood, these individuals were known to be dependent on other's approval and displaying a lack of confidence (Feeney et al., 1994). Moreover, insecurely attached individuals were obsessed with relationships and regularly expressed feelings of powerlessness (Kobak, Sudler, & Gamble, 1992). Individuals categorized as insecure-ambivalent, are known to retain a negative view of themselves and positive views of others (Feeney et al., 1994). Finally, extremely abnormal infant behaviors and adult patterns of speech were observed for the classification of disorganized attachment, that can also be a sub-classification of other attachment classifications or stand alone. The unusual behaviors were noted to occur during stressful situations. For instance, as a reaction to stress infants would freeze in place or suddenly lay on the floor (Main, 1996). Infants classified with disorganized attachment behavior have been associated with adults who have unconsciously mistreated them. These infants may behave aggressively in childhood (Lyons-Ruth & Block, 1996). In adulthood, they can suffer from a range of psychological problems (Lyons-Ruth & Block, 1996). Bowlby pointed out that one's gender was not a deterrent from attachment problems.

In Bowlby's theory of attachment, gender classifications were not included. This was most likely due to the fact that the need for protection is not gender specific, as both male and female infants need parents who respond and protect them (Simpson, 1999; Mercer, 2006). Gender differences was identified in a study conducted by Del Giudice (2008) which utilized a story completion task called the Manchester Child Attachment Story Task with both male and female in middle childhood from six to seven years of age. This study revealed a difference between gender and specific insecure attachment behavior patterns. Similar to the above distribution a difference was discovered within the secure subtypes albeit it was determined to be weaker. Moreover, the data confirmed prior observations that found higher disorganization in men. However, many other researchers have reported no gender differences with regard to attachment classifications. For instance, Bakersmans-Kranenburg and van Ijzendoorn (2009) attempted to duplicate the above research of middle childhood boys and girls and their studied revealed no gender differences with respect to attachment patterns.

The internal working model and other aspects of Bowlby's attachment theory received lots of attention during its time, because it went in direct opposition to what many believed. One such critic of his theory was Sigmund Freud, as he was considered to be one of the authority figures on attachment. A brief summation of his and other disciplines views will be explained in the next section.

Controversy. Bowlby's attachment theory elicited controversy in many disciplines, including psychoanalysis, ethology, cognitive development, and behaviorism. From its conception, there was censure because the theory was not consistent with the fractioning branches of psychoanalysis. Although Bowlby is known as the founder of the attachment theory, Sigmund Freud, the father of psychoanalytical theory, was the first to speak about attachment between mother and child in his developmental stage theory. Freud (1989) framed his theory around the psyche, which he explained as being "mental life" (p.13). Freud theorized that behavior patterns of dependency develop in early childhood for survival, as the child is solely depended on its mother to properly feed and nurture him. Freud felt that if the attachment between the child and mother is prematurely severed or the child's needs are excessively attended, the child would become an adult who would be overly dependent on others to satisfy his needs.

Though Bowlby was a classically trained psychoanalyst, he felt that this psychoanalytical view was very narrowed and outdated. He argued that attachment behavior was not as simplified as Freud and other psychoanalysts believed. Bowlby postulated that this behavior was not the product of the need to satisfy one's desires, but a separate entity, that should be viewed by itself and considered equally important to human nature (Bowlby, 1973).

At the time Bowlby entered into the psychoanalytical realm, there were two competing factions within the British Psychoanalytical Society and he disagreed with both. In one branch, psychoanalyst Melanie Klein proposed that the infant had a fundamental object relation to the mother and had a psychic life ruled by sadistic fantasies and aggression, deriving from the death instinct (Hall, 2007; Holmes, 1993). The other branch was ruled by Anna Freud; much like her father, she embraced the drive theory and held the view that there was an unconscious instinctive drive, which was motivated to attach to objects in order to evade unhappiness (Zepf, Zepf, & Turnbull, 2006). Bowlby disagreed with both hypotheses and felt that further investigation was necessary in order to fully understand attachment and its impact on infants. Bowlby disagreed with both hypotheses and felt that further investigation was necessary in order to fully understand attachment and its impact on infants. He felt that both branches failed to understand the true nature of attachment. Bowlby's inability to align with either branch left him vulnerable to criticism by prominent scholars in his field. Consequently, during his time, members of his community ignored him and did not view his ideas as credible. He argued against the belief that an infant's attachment to an adult was simply related to satisfying one's basic physiological needs (Zepf et al., 2006). Likewise, he believed that the drive theory missed the mark, as he disagreed with the use of needs being a motivational force. He explained that needs are not a behavioral system and cannot activate a behavioral system; they can only dictate the function of the behavioral system (Zepf et al., 2006).

However, Bowlby was ahead of his time and realized that findings from other scientific branches have insight into attachment theory. Ethology is the scientific study of animal behavior and was introduced by Konrad Lorenz and Niko Tinbergen in the 1930s. Bowlby was one of the first people to recognize and incorporate this approach into a psychological theory, as he came to believe that there was a direct relation to animal behavior and human behavior. However, some ethologists questioned Bowlby's use of ethology in attachment theory, as they argued that his theory focused on older versions of the ethological approach and failed to recognize and include advances in this field (Schur, 1960). Others argued that no single behavior can be attributed to attachment behavior only, but must be viewed in its context. Moreover, the two main components of the attachment theory, protesting and proximity seeking, are symptomatic of the level of attachment and are arranged with regard to context and behavior; therefore, should not be viewed simply as evolutionary components (Sroufe & Waters, 1977). Furthermore, due to infants' inability to explain their emotions, it is argued that many components like crying and smiling, are impossible to measure; therefore, they cannot definitively be attributed to evolutionary instinct. For example, the length of time an infant cries after departure of caregiver has been associated with the level of attachment between infant and child in Bowlby's theory. However, it is stipulated that there could be numerous contextual factors that might encourage the infant to cry, such as the child's emotional and mental level, fatigue, and physical wellbeing (Sroufe & Waters, 1977). Likewise, there are some concerns with regard to aspects of Bowlby's internal working model theory, as it is has become a catch-all used to explain away a variety of psychological issues (Hinde & Stevenson-Hinde, 1993).

Bowlby (1969) strayed away from the traditional psychoanalytical theory and the other disciplines and attempted to elucidate behavior and psychopathology in a more developmental, prospective fashion. He highlighted in his writings that attachment is fundamentally an empirically testable theory that is ethologically and biologically based, that includes a variety of psychological constructs (Bowlby, 1969). He further postulated that attachment was not a fleeting concept, but rather a lifelong one, as all members of the infant species exhibit attachment behaviors toward their primary attachment figures (Bowlby, 1969). Bowlby (1969) hypothesized that there was an indirect link to pathology and attachment behavior. Dysfunctional attachment relationships in childhood have a significant influence on development and attachment behavior in adulthood, as adult attachment behavior is a direct extension and continuation of attachment behavior that occurred during childhood. He argued that there are definite types of attachment behaviors that are responsible for destructive relationship patterns that are associated with other types of psychopathology like depression.

Although, Bowlby's attachment theory received criticism from some of his colleagues, some felt that his theory deserved more attention. Mary Ainsworth was one of those people and she will be discussed in the next section.

Ainsworth's Attachment Theory

Ainsworth (1919-1999), a developmental psychologist, was essential in presenting to the world a much more complex conceptualization of the attachment theory. Ainsworth became a prominent figure in the psychological arena after her first study of the interactions between mother and child in Uganda. This study was important, because it led to the realization that the parent-child relationship evolved from the basic, visual behaviors of clinging and crying, which was originally introduced by Bowlby, to more complex affective communication in which both mother and child must participate (Ainsworth, 1978). This was a noteworthy finding, because if the mother was not receptive and sensitive to the infant's affective cues, the probability of the child suffering from an attachment disorder was believed to be heightened (Lyons-Ruth, 2006). In the Strange Situation study, which will be described in detail later, Ainsworth and her colleagues researched and observed the construction of the development of infant connection to the mothers, and the mothers as the secure base, which allowed the newborns the security to discover the world around them. The child's attachment to the mother was measured by the mother's responses to the infants' cues, i.e., "differential crying, smiling, and vocalization" (Ainsworth, Blehar, Wall, & Waters, 1978, p. 88).

Finally, Ainsworth's studies led to the determination that a mother figure does not necessitate an attachment figure, as some of the children in her studies from Uganda displayed attachment to other members of their family (Ainsworth, Blehar, Walls &

Waters, 1978). A child in the first year of life chooses his principal attachment figure by

attaching to whoever takes on the main role of caregiver in the household. The more an

infant engages with another person, the stronger the attachment to that individual;

therefore, it was determined that the attachment role can effectively be taken on by other

people besides a mother (Bowlby, 1982). In most cultures a mother, father, older siblings,

and sometimes grandparents are placed in this role. However, the primary attachment

figure is usually the mother, as she is normally charged with the care of the infant. The

secondary attachment figure in a child's life is often the father, as the father is commonly

the one who would take on the caregiver role when the mother is not available. It is

important to note that most people have several attachment figures by the time they reach

one year of age.

The strange situation. The Strange Situation is an experimental setup in which

the reaction of and infant is studied when it is left by the mother in the care of a stranger

and upon reunion with the mother. This study was instrumental in the previous discussed

classification of attachment behaviors of adult and infant attachment behaviors. As

discussed above, infant attachment behaviors are classified as secure, insecure-avoidant,

insecure-ambivalent, and disorganized (Main, 1996). Adult attachment behaviors are

named slightly different: secure, autonomous, insecure-dismissing, insecure-preoccupied,

and unresolved-disorganized. See Table 1 for a comparison between adult and child

attachment styles. Here we will focus on the child attachment.

In the strange situation, the infants were placed in groups according to their observed responses when separated for 15 minutes from their mothers. Group A infants were known as *anxious-avoidant*. Group B infants were classified as *secure* and group C infants were categorized as *insecure-resistant/anxious-ambivalent*. From this study, Ainsworth and her colleagues observed healthy and positive attachment interactions between the infants and mothers in the secure Group B. It was noted that the mothers in this category had equipped their children with the necessary amount of confidence to feel safe, which allowed them to experience little anxiety outside of the presence of their secure base, the mother.

However, participants in group A were classified as being *insecure-avoidant* and were observed to exhibit little need for comfort and physical contact by the mother after the 15 minute separation period. They were described as, emotionally distant, rejecting, and did not interact well with the other children (Ainsworth et al., 1978). In times of distress or discomfort, infants in this stage were observed not to have a preferential response to their mother, as they would allow either a stranger or their mother to engage with them. It is believed that children who have *anxious-avoidant* attachment behaviors might be subject to repetitive rejection from their own mothers or caregivers, which activates defensive mechanisms; namely, disconnection and avoidance in order to effectively cope with the rejection (Bowlby, 1980). Avoidance and disconnection behaviors serve to lessen or make tolerable the pain that is initiated by the mother's or caregiver's failure or inability to act upon the needs of the child. As a result, the child may become numb to affection behaviors by the caregiver or anyone else who might attempt to comfort the child.

The third, group C, *insecure-resistant/anxious-ambivalent*, infants exhibited extreme anxiety upon the departure of the mothers. Upon being reunited with their mothers, the infants were not receptive to attempts to comfort them. The researchers observed an unusual amount of internal conflict among the infants in group C with regard to the perceived emotional and physical availability of the mother (Ainsworth et al., 1978). As a result of this experience with group C, the researchers hypothesized that patterns of interaction between mother and child were linked to the amount of responsiveness the mother initiated toward the child. It was theorized by Ainsworth and Bowlby that mother and child have a dyadic relationship, which only works if the mother and child participate equally. If the child feels that the attachment figure is not emotionally or physically available, the child will not believe in the safety of his secure base and consequently he will experience heighten anxiety (Ainsworth, Blehar, Walls, & Waters, 1978; Bowlby, 1973; Peluso, Peluso, White & Kern, 2004). Fear behavior and attachment behavior are cohesive behaviors that are triggered by the same circumstances (Ainsworth, 1967). These behaviors are activated in times of danger or the potential threat of danger. If a child believes that he is in danger, he will seek proximity to the attachment figure. A dysfunctional parent-child relationship may arise if the caregivers are emotionally and physically unattainable causing them to be unable to provide the child with security they desire.

Table 1

Adult Attachment Classifications and Strange Situation Categories

Adult Attachment Interview	Infant Strange Situation Response
Dismissing (Ds). Normalizing, positive descriptions of parents are unsupported or contradicted by specific memories. Negative experiences said to have had no effect. Transcripts are short, often with insistence on lack of memory.	Avoidant (A). Does not cry on separation, attending toys or environment throughout procedure. Actively avoids and ignores parent on reunion, moving away, turning away, or leaning away when picked up. Unemotional; expressions of anger are absent.
Secure-autonomous (F). Coherent, collaborative discourse is maintained during description and evaluation of attachment-related experiences, whether these experiences are described as favorable or unfavorable. Speaker seems to value attachment while being objective regarding any particular experience.	Secure (B). Shows signs of missing parent on first separation and cries during second separation. Greets parent actively; for example, creeping to parent at once, seeking to be held. After briefly maintaining contact with the parent, settles, and returns to play.
Preoccupied (E). Preoccupied with experiences, seeming angry, confused and passive, or fearful and overwhelmed. Some sentences grammatically entangled or filled with vague phrases. Transcripts are long, some responses irrelevant.	Resistant-ambivalent (C). Preoccupied with parent throughout procedure, may seem actively angry alternately seeking and resisting parent, or may be passive. Fails to return to settle or return to exploration on reunion and continues to focus on parent and cry.
Unresolved-disorganized (U-d). During discussions of loss or abuse, shows striking lapse in the monitoring of reasoning or discourse: for example, may speak of the dead person as if still alive in the physical sense, fall silent, or use eulogistic speech. May otherwise fit well in Ds, F, or E category.	Disorganized-disoriented (D). Disorganized or disoriented behaviors displayed in parent's presence; for example, may freeze with a trance-like expression, hands in air, rise and then fall prone at parent's entrance, or cling while leaning away. May otherwise fit well to A, B, or C category.

Note. Adapted from "Introduction for the Special Edition on Attachment and Psychopathology: Overview of the Field of Attachment," by M. Main, 1996, *Journal of Consulting and Clinical Psychology*, 64, p. 237-243.

Measuring Attachment

Bowlby's introduction of attachment theory to the psychological arena spurred research to test his theory. By utilizing observed infant behavior's demonstrated in Ainsworth's Strange Situation study; they were able to further operationalize attachment behavior in adults and develop validated self-reported measures (Del Giudice, 2009; see Ainsworth, 1973; see Hesse, 1999). Due to these early pioneers, attachment behavior has become a measurable theoretical concept, which has attracted long-term interest into the implications of attachment across the life span (Del Giudice, 2009). Below I will first discuss common measures of adult attachment and next common measures of child attachment.

Adult Attachment Interview. The Adult Attachment Interview (AAI) is a structured set of questions which allows a researcher to determine attachment patterns present in an adult or adolescent (Hesse, 1999). The individual being assessed reports their experiences of attachment during childhood and ways these may have influenced their adult behavior and personality. The AAI includes a coding system which is used to classify the individual (Hesse, 1999).

The AAI is designed in a semi-structured interview format. It contains 15 principal questions, which includes supplementary probes governed by interviewers who were trained in this area. The questions surround experiences in childhood, such as details about relationships during childhood, feelings and experiences regarding any rejections, loss, trauma and abuse that may have occurred during childhood, and questions relating to present relationships and current parental relational changes (Hesse,

1999). The interviews are normally transcribed verbatim and scored and classified. Currently, the AAI coding scale consists of several scales that are scored in a 9-point system with a final classification. The AAI coders utilize a variety of scales that are connected to each parent and childhood experiences, including rejection and loving experiences. Moreover, the coders use a code 7 scale "states of mind," that will be included in the discussion below. This scale is essential, as the last classification was mainly based on scores from the states of mind scales (Hesse, 1999). Hesse (1999) made available a synopsis of attachment classifications and related state of mind scales. (See Table 2.)

A strength of the AAI is that it has been used for over 25 years (Horowitz & Strack, 2011). This has allowed the instrument to be tested and validated extensively. It has excellent external validation and has repeatedly demonstrated its ability to accurately predict interviewee's classifications of responses regarding attachment. It also overlaps well with a variety of constructs regarding attachment such as those related to romantic attraction. It should be noted that the AAI is not a major of romance but focuses on attachments in the nuclear family (Horowitz & Strack, 2011).

A major weakness of the AAI is that it is an interview (Hesse, 1999). There are a variety of factors which could influence an individual to give inaccurate results. For example, the individual may report how they believe they should respond in attachment situations rather than the way they actually respond. Also, people are notoriously inaccurate when reporting aspects of their own behavior and personality. In other words, the person may simply report incorrect information (Hesse, 1999).

Experiences in Close Relationships. The Experiences in Close Relationships -

Revised (ECR-R) questionnaire is another method of measuring adult attachment (Fraley,

Waller & Brennan, 2000). This is a 36 item questionnaire developed through factor

analysis of previously existing self-report measures related to adult romantic attachment.

This questionnaire yields the subscales of anxiety and avoidance. These 2 dimensions

yield 4 categories (Fraley, Waller & Brennan, 2000).

A major strength of the ECR-R is that it was derived from a large number of self

report measures which already existed (Fraley, Waller, & Brennan, 2000). A factor

analysis was done on the results in order to develop the instrument. This type of analysis

makes it more likely that the questionnaire describes underlying factors which exist over

a number of studies. This increases the likelihood of the measure having external validity

(Fraley, Waller, & Brennan, 2000).

A weakness of the ECR-R is similar to the AAI (Fraley, Waller, & Brennan,

2000). Individuals are answering a questionnaire about their attachments. While it is less

likely that they will give answers which they perceive to be favorable in a questionnaire

as opposed to an interview, is still quite possible. Also, the problem remains of people

being able to accurately perceive matters regarding their own behavior or personality

(Fraley, Waller, & Brennan, 2000).

Strange Situation. The previously discussed Strange Situation is the most

common method for assessing the attachment which is empirically supported. The

instrument was originally developed by Ainsworth et al. (1978) for research purposes. It

was not designed as a diagnostic tool. The procedure consists of placing an infant and his/her mother in an unfamiliar room filled with toys. The researcher observes through a one-way mirror and records reactions. There are 8 episodes which consists of the mother being separated from the baby and reunited in 3 minutes or less. The reaction of the intent upon being reunited with their mother is the basis for the classification of attachment (Ainsworth et al., 1978).

The strange situation assessment has been used for over 30 years and has been shown to be a reliable predictor of attachment tendencies (Horowitz & Strack, 2011). It has also been shown to be accurate in cross-sectional studies. The attachment classifications correlate well with the quality and quantity of peer relationships. Higher correlations are reached regarding close relationships. Children who are secure are likely to have higher quality friendships with a larger number of individuals. Children who are found to be insecure and attachments are likely to be followers rather than leaders (Horowitz & Strack, 2011).

The strange situation has its weaknesses as a method of assessing attachment (Horowitz & Strack, 2011). The brief separation and reunion between infant and mother is assumed to have the same meaning for all of the children being tested. However, the likelihood of separation within a culture can make a substantial difference regarding its interpretation by infants. For example, infants and Japan are almost never separated from their mothers. The experience may prove more traumatic for these infants regardless of their attachment pattern. Additionally, the test is used to measure attachment and children who are 12 to 20 months of age. Children who are 20 months of age are significantly more cognitively advanced than a 12-month-old. These older infants may not find experience a traumatic due to the cognitive ability to understand that the mother is likely to return (Horowitz & Strack, 2011).

Disturbances of Attachment Interview. The Disturbances of Attachment Interview (DAI) is a semi-structured interview which is given to caregivers by clinicians to investigate items related to an infant's attachments (Mower, Robinson, & Lasik, 2009). There 12 questions guiding this interview: seeks comfort when distressed, has a preferred adult, respond well to comforting, level of emotional regulation, social reciprocity, anxiety with unfamiliar adults, checking when away from caregiver, reaction to strangers, level of self endangering behavior, role reversal, vigilance, and clinging behavior (Mower, Robinson, & Lasik, 2009).

Strength of the DAI is that it has been standardized for the diagnosis of reactive attachment disorder (Mower, Robinson, & Lasik, 2009). This disorder results in disturbed social relationships. As a consequence the child is often not able to respond appropriately or initiate social interactions. These children are inhibited in a variety of social situations (Mower, Robinson, & Lasik, 2009).

Weaknesses of the DAI are the same as for any interview-based technique (Mower, Robinson, & Lasik, 2009). The interviewer must rely upon being given accurate information by the interviewee. The individual being interviewed may choose to provide information which they believe will be acceptable rather than accurate. Also, the interviewer can inadvertently influence the types of answers which are provided (Mower, Robinson, & Lasik, 2009).

In conclusion, researchers have classified attachment for both adults and infants. Infant attachment behavior is most commonly measured through the use of the Strange Situation and adult attachment behaviors is commonly conducted with the Adult Attachment Interview (AAI). These two measures remain the most popular means of measuring attachment behaviors (Main, 1996). Due to the difficulty of administering and scoring the Adult Attachment Interview, researchers have created other objective self-report assessments that are useful to measure attachment in adolescent and adults (de Haas, Bakermans-Kranenburg, & Van ljzendoorm, 1994). Finding an appropriate tool to measure attachment is important in order to accurately classify attachment propensities in society. The next section will provide a breakdown of attachment classifications in the United States.

Dissemination of Attachment Classifications in Society

Clinical studies have shown that 60% of the middle class in the United States had scored consistently in the secure attachment range, and approximately 20% was in the avoidant category, and 10% was within the resistant group, and 10 to 15 % of the overall population was classified into the disorganized grouping (Colin, 1996). However, the results from clinical studies discovered a different distribution, as these researchers reported a larger percentage of people were classified in the insecure range. These clinical studies revealed less than 10% in the secure range, 25% dismissing and 25% preoccupied, and 40% in the unresolved and disorganized category (Crowell, Fraley, & Shaver, 1999). One particular studied discovered that change in caregiving environment, such as parental death, divorce, and serious illnesses was linked with substantial change in the caregiving environment (Crowell & Waters, 2005). As a result, these traumatic

events were responsible for only one-third of secure children, who had experienced one

or more traumatic event, remained secure in adulthood; whereas 85% of secure children

who did not suffer a traumatic event in childhood remained secure in adulthood (Crowell

& Waters, 2005).

Table 2

Summation of States of Mind Scales Equated with Attachment Classification

Dismissing (Ds)	Secure (F)	Preoccupied (E)
Scale: Idealization of attachment figures	Scale: Coherence of Transcript	Scale: Involved/involving anger toward attachment figures
General descriptions of the parent are not consistent with the reader's inference of parental behavior, including overly positive descriptions or overt contradictions between descriptions and inferred experience present.	There are few violations of Grice's maxims of coherent communication, quantity, quality, relation, and manner. The interviewee presents a steadily flowing development and freshness of speech that presents a unified, non-contradictory, and complete impression of childhood experiences with parents and the effects of those experiences.	Speech that includes run-on, entangled sentences that list offenses of the parent or angrily addressing parent during the interview would receive high ratings on this scale. Simple statements of anger toward the parent do not necessarily receive high ratings.
Scale: Insistence on Lack of Memory for Childhood Interviewee responds to interview questions with "I don't know," which serves to block discourse.	Scale: Metacognitive monitoring Style of active monitoring of discourse that indicates ability to identify and correct contradictions, perceive differences in perceptions over time and with respect to different persons and their perspectives.	Scale: Passivity or vagueness in discourse The interviewee seems unable to find words or focus on the interview topic, such that nonsense words are used, or pronoun confusion between the self and the parent appear in the transcript. The interviewee may also slip into childlike speech, as if absorbed in childhood memories.
Scale: Derogating dismissal of attachment Cool, contemptuous dismissal of relationships and their importance, such that attachment-related experiences are considered foolish or beneath consideration.		

Attachment Stability over Time

The above section provided an explanation of attachment classifications. This section will build upon that discussion by explaining whether or not a person suffering from a particular attachment classification will continue to suffer from this disorder over time. The literature search did not reveal unequivocal evidence for the stability of attachment over the lifespan. Crowell and Waters (2005) advised that attachment representations remain stable across circumstances. They further highlighted that there are few studies which empirically supports attachment stability over time. Other researchers have also postulated that attachment classifications remain relatively constant for individuals over time (Colin,1996; Grossmann, K.E., Grossmann, K., & Zimmermann, P., 1999; van IJzendoorn & Bakersmans-Kranenberg, 1997). Attachment consistency over time has been connected with the stability of one's environment (Grossmann et al., 1999). One's views surrounding attachment relationships are developed from consistent attachment interactions over time. It is highly probable that one will draw from past experience in order to make strategic decisions through the life span (Colin, 1996; Del Giudice, 2009; van Ijzendoorm & Bakersmans-Kranenberg,1997). For instance, caregiving environments that are reliably receptive and sensitive or environments that are constantly negligent and insensitive have a high probability of one's internalization of those attachment experiences (Colin, 1996; Del Giudice, 2009; van Ijzendoorm & Bakersmans-Kranenberg,1997). One's attachment classifications could alter if the caregiving environment or attachment figure's obtainability alters significantly (Colin, 1996; van Ijzendoorm & Bakersmans-Kranenberg, 1997). Generally, middle-class environments and various other constant environments have displayed superior stability with regard to maintaining attachments over time (Weinfield, Sroufe, Egeland, & Carlson, 1999). An examination of empirical studies of stability overtime was presented by Hesse (1999). Through the use of Adult samples, the Adult Attachment Interview found stability over time to be suitable utilizing a three-category classification (secure, dismissing, and preoccupied) for test-retest spans of three months to four years (see Hesse, 1999).

Depression and Attachment

Hypothesized Connections between Attachment and Depression

As explained above, attachment classifications are linked to one's home environment and may continue across the lifespan. The insecure attachment category has been connected to various forms of psychopathology, such as anxiety and depression (Allen, Hauser, & Borman-Spurrell, 1996; Armsden, McCauley, Greenberg, Burke, Mitchell, 1990; Brumariu & Kerns, 2010). It is important to note that secure attachment was seen as a safeguard against the majority of emotional suffering and researchers did not believe that insecure attachment patterns would cause or directly foretell depression propensities (Cummings & Cicchetti, 1990; Roberts, Gotlib, & Kassel, 1996).

Cicchetti, Toth, and Lyncy (1995) explained that insecurely attached people were likely to be predisposed to develop depression, as it was hypothesized that they had fewer coping methods available to handle stress due to the lack of felt security and their self-schema of being unlovable or undesirable. The link between depression and attachment has been hypothesized to originate from inconsistent care giving by attachment figures

(Cole-Detke & Kobak, 1996). For instance, children who experience inconsistent care giving might become hyper vigilant to their caregiver in order to increase their chance to receive nurturing. Consequently, this hyper vigilant behavior might serve as a distraction and stop the child from his exploration of his environment and cause the child to become excessively attentive to others (Cole-Detke & Kobak, 1996). Moreover, the inconsistent behavior of the attachment figures' response could cause the child to have low self-esteem, become fixated on their believed faults, and create a worldview of hopelessness (Cole-Detke & Kobak, 1996). Beck (1967) concurred with this theory, as he proposed that depression is the result of negative thought patterns that are formed from a dysfunctional belief system. He further found that the loss of a parental figure in childhood is a catalyst for the development of a negative belief system; therefore, would be a significant contributor to the development of depression in adulthood. A direct link to the type of attachment a child has with their parental figures has been identified with depression (Liu, 2007).

However, not all insecure attachment styles indicate a higher incidence of depression. Some attachment classifications were linked to depression and others to other psychiatric diagnoses. A study among college women (Cole-Detke & Kobak, 1996) found that participants whose attachment styles was categorized as preoccupied were most likely to report depressive symptoms; whereas participants who were categorized as dismissing were most commonly reporting other psychiatric disorders such as eating disorder symptoms, instead of depression symptoms (Cole-Detke & Kobak, 1996). Another study involving adolescent psychiatric patients (Rosenstein & Horowitz, 1996) also observed that certain psychiatric diagnoses, such as conduct disorder or substance abuse disorder were associated with a dismissing attachment style, while a preoccupied attachment style was associated with major depression, dysthymia, or schizoaffective disorder. A study of urban adolescents (Kobak, Sudler, & Gamble, 1992) also found that a preoccupied attachment style has a probability of reporting depressive symptoms. This was especially true for the male participants. However, the female participants were also at increased risk for depression if they had a dismissing attachment style (Kobak et al., 1992). Thus preoccupied behavioral strategies are highly associated with depression. It has been suggested that this may be due to heighten feelings of helplessness and frustration, which have been correlated with depression (Kobak et al., 1992).

Contrary to the positive results discussed above. A study among inpatient adults discovered no correlation between depression and attachment classifications; however, some of the findings might have been misidentified due to high comorbidity of psychological diagnoses (Fonagy et al., 1996). Even though no correlation was found among diagnoses and attachment, patterns were found present for diagnoses and scales in the AAI. For instance, adults who were diagnosed as depressed scored the lowest in idealization and the highest on the anger classification scale. These study results were unclear to determine whether unipolar depression was correlated with attachment classifications; however, there might be an association between diagnoses and exact rating scales used in the AAI. The authors proposed that in order to arrive at an accurate determination there needs to be more research of depression in correlation to attachment classification (Fonagy et al., 1996).

A meta-analysis was inconclusive with regard to whether there was a correlation between attachment and depression (van IJzendoorn & Bakermans-Kranenburg, 1996). The meta-analysis included mothers, fathers, and adolescents and the researchers concluded that there was an over-representation of adults in clinical groups who were classified as insecure. However, it was noted that not many of the studies included in the meta-analysis specifically investigated psychiatric diagnoses. For example, van IJezendoorn and Bakermans-Kranenburg's meta-analysis reported that researchers in one study found correlations with dysthymic disorder and dismissing attachment classification, which is considered to be an insecure attachment (see Patrick, Hobson, Castle, Howard, & Maughan, 1994). Another investigation found a relationship with preoccupied attachment classification and unipolar depression (Rosentstein & Horowitz, 1993). These investigators emphasized that there is a need for more research of psychological symptoms and diagnoses in correlation to attachment classifications (van IJzendoorn & Bakermans-Kranenburg, 1996). Even though there were no consistent result that found correlations between attachment and diagnoses, there were some consistent results that led researchers to conclude, through experiences with caregivers, attachment classifications are in some fashion linked with risk factors for specific forms of emotional suffering. Pathways, such as cognitive vulnerabilities and internal working models, are believed to be associated with attachment and depression has not been fully researched.

Parental separation and depression. As discussed above, attachment

difficulties may occur when parents are unavailable as a caregiver. Insecure attachment

may have negative long-term consequences for the child, who believes loved ones will be

unavailable in times of stress and need. This may lead to feelings of hopelessness and

helplessness. Amato (1991) discovered a direct relationship to parental absence and adult

depression. He observed a higher prevalence of depression among Caucasian and

African-American participants who suffered the loss of a parent during childhood. There

was no such effect found on Hispanic men or females. Additionally, the study revealed

that African-Americans were the most negatively impacted by the absence of a parent

compared to the other ethnic/racial groups.

Amato's findings were not surprising, as it is believed that parental bonds assist in

the development of self-worth and one's ability to trust and love others (Kenny & Sirin,

2006). Moreover, one's self-concepts are generated during childhood and are derived

from one's experiences, beliefs, and attachment with their parents (Beck, 1967). It is

further hypothesized that a child who loses a parent or caregiver would internalize the

loss and come to believe that other attachment figures would behave in the same manner

(Bowlby, 1973). Accordingly, this type of loss could hinder a child's ability to develop

attachments to others and cause that child to develop negative self-judgments; if

untreated could lead to depression (Beck, 1967; Bowlby, 1982). The research has led to

the conclusion that a traumatic loss in one's family environment could elicit childhood

depression (Ainsworth, 2000). It is further pontificated that childhood and adolescent

depression could be detrimental, as it is a persistent disorder that has great potential to re-occur later in life. A limitation to Amato's study was that the researcher was unable to delineate why African-American participants displayed higher levels of depression in adulthood than the other participants.

Further literature suggested that children who are reared in a single-mother headed household are more likely than a child reared in a two-parent headed household with their biological father to experience depression (Beaty, 1995). It is hypothesized that the loss of an attachment relationship, such as a biological attachment figure, during childhood could cause a child to mourn the loss and consequently, the child may feel abandoned, helpless, unwanted, and unloved (Sloman, Price, Gilbert, & Gardner, 1994). Rejection by a primary attachment figure during childhood has been equated with depressive symptoms, as the child may develop negative self-view of themselves and the world around them (Oliver, 2003). If the child does not receive assistance in dealing with these feelings, this child could develop a depressive disorder that would remain with him well into adulthood (Rohde, Lewinsohn, & Sedey, 1990).

It is proposed that an unhealthy childhood experience with a primary attachment figure encourages feelings of helplessness, which is a learned behavior (Seligman, 1992). A child learns early on that he has the ability to control his environment. For instance, when a child cries he initiates a response from his caregiver and in time the child comes to expect changes to occur in the environment in response to his behavior. If his behavior does not elicit a change, helplessness and depression develop (Seligman, 1992). In the event of the loss of a primary attachment figure, the child's inability to preserve the relationship causes him to feel helpless and experience chronic mourning. It was pontificated that men who were abandoned by their father grieve the loss of the paternal figure and consequently have a higher propensity to develop depression, which could continue into adulthood (Balcom, 1998).

As discussed above the loss of an attachment figure can cause a child to suffer attachment problems and depression in adulthood. Researchers conducted a study that sought to determine whether gender would play a role on how one reacted to being separated from an attachment figure. Maier and Lachman (2000) discovered that male participants who were separated from a parent before the age of 17 due to divorce displayed lower levels of self-acceptance, poorer relations with others, increased levels of both acute and chronic health problems and increased depression. These findings suggest that relative to men, women appear to suffer less when separated from a parent due to divorce during their childhood. In fact, there was no significant effect on women's psychological well-being in the Maier and Lachman study. However, women whose parents divorced did report higher levels of health problems. A limitation to this study was that it failed to identify consequences of gender-to-gender separation, in particular the separation between the paternal figure and the male child and its impact on the adult child. Another limitation was that it did not identify the impact of separation of an attachment figure on different racial categories. Also, this study did not discuss the internal working model and how it too can be negatively impacted by parental separation. In conclusion, there is evidence that breaking of parental attachment during childhood can cause a child to suffer from depression in adulthood particularly in African-American men. In conclusion, attachment starts in infancy and is relatively stable through childhood, and insecure attachment raises the risk for depression in adulthood. However, a discussion of attachment would not be complete without addressing criticism.

Critiques of Attachment Theory

Attachment theory is not without its critics. One criticism of the theory is that parents will nearly always produce children who have similar traits (Lee, 2003). This is assumed to be true because the parents shape the personality of the child (Lee, 2003). However, this does not take into account the influence of peers. A peer group can have a significant influence on a child as well and may be quite different from their parents (Lee, 2003). There are often social factors at work which encourage children to blend in with their peers more than their own family (Lee, 2003). Thus, attachment could be theorized to be shaped as much by infant-mother relationships as by peer relationships later in life.

Another limitation of attachment theory is that it is based on the behavior of an infant during a brief separation from their mother (Lee, 2003). However, these separations are only brief and can be considered as temporary stressful situations. They may be better representative of how the infant deals with stress rather than its attachment to the mother (Lee, 2003). Furthermore, these short separations may not be representative of the way the child interacts with other loved ones in their social environment to whom the child is attached (Benson & Haith, 2009). For example, if the primary attachment figure is a mother the child may cry upon separation. However, upon separation from a grandmother there may only be slight anxiety with no crying (Benson & Haith, 2009).

While there is some acknowledgment that the primary attachment figure could be someone other than the mother, there is little recognition that the same type of attachment may exist between another individual such as an aunt, uncle, or sibling (Benson & Haith, 2009). This neglects the reality that most adults have several primary attachments. This leads to the limitation created by the attachment model focusing primarily on early childhood and infancy (Benson & Haith, 2009). This limitation may cause other researchers to falsely negate other attachment figures roles in a child's life and impact studies that follow them into adulthood.

Attachment Literature Summary

Bowlby (1982) designed the attachment theory to explain behaviors initiated by young children, after being separated from their mother, as this appeared to be linked to the emotional wellbeing of a child. The purpose of attachment behavior is to maintain security to an attachment figure (children to parents or adults to romantic partners) in times of believed danger across one's lifespan (Bowlby, 1982). The internal working model is one of the main components of the attachment theory. It is responsible for guiding one's behaviors and expectations in regards to attachment (Bowlby, 1973) and it also serves as a means to conceptualize the self and others (Bowlby, 1980; Griffith, 2004; Mercer, 2006). In theory, the internal working model was believed to be constructed by one's cognition, as it serves as an outline of expectations and information. This information is assimilated, stored, and responsible for influencing one's beliefs, interactions and behaviors with new attachment figures.

Many authors have presupposed that children with healthy internal models had primary attachment figures who were sensitive and responsive to their needs during times of stress (Mikulincer, Shaver, Sapir-Lavid, & Avihou-Kanza, 2009). Low levels of positive parental interaction was said to heighten the child's risk of negative outcomes during adolescents and adulthood (Chester, Jones, Zalot, & Sterret, 2007). The self-schema and external schema formed by these negative and positive attachment experiences during childhood play an essential role in how one view's themselves and the world around them (Bretherton, 1990). During adulthood the information within the internal model varies and can be divided into four primary adult attachment classifications (Bretherton, 1990). For instance, individuals classified as dismissing (Ds) may be vigilant in their self-schema of independence, while maintaining the belief that others may fail to respond effectively to their needs (Bretherton & Munholland, 1999). In contrast, individuals that are secure (F) might hold internal working model content that supports their schema that they are worthy to receive support from others and that they can depend on others to be available when they are stressed (Priel & Shamai, 1995). Finally, individuals classified as preoccupied (E) may have self-schemas that tell them they are not worthy of support and that no one would be available to help them during times of need. Their self-schema would consist of a negative representation of themselves and a positive representation of others (Carnelly et al., 1994).

This theory maybe true for many incarcerated adult African-American men, who were raised in father-absent homes, research has found that African-American men raised in these environments are more likely to be incarcerated (Bush, Mullis, & Mullis, 2000; Harper & McLanahan, 2004). It is this study's desire to determine whether paternal absence may cause African-American men to suffer from attachment and depression difficulties in adulthood; if there is a correlation, it may serve to high light an unrecognized problem that may account for the high number of incarcerated African-American men.

Implications for Adult African-American Men

This research is necessary, because there is a high preponderance of children growing up without their fathers in single-parent homes. African-American children are more likely than Caucasian and Hispanic children to live in a mother headed single-parent home. In 2011, 65% of African-American children lived in a single-parent home without a paternal figure present (FIFCFS, 2012).

Although women are usually the primary caregiver and attachment person of the child, men with absent fathers are known to experience difficulty with attachment relationships. It was discovered in a study conducted by Caldera (2004) that fathers who were involved in caring for their infants were reported to raise children who were socially competent and self-secure. The quality of parental interaction with the child has been determined to predict how the child views their current and future relationships with other attachment figures (Liu, 2007). Even when one parent provides adequate attachment, the loss of attachment with another parent may cause children to develop self-doubt and the inability to trust others. Consequently, if the individual does not receive help with these feelings, depression may become an issue for them. Ainsworth (2000) points out "childhood depression is familial; episodes of depression are triggered by emotionally traumatic losses" (p. 25). Childhood and adolescent depression can be detrimental, as it is persistent and also can re-occur later in life.

Another factor contributing to depression in single-parent homes is the fact that a large portion of these homes suffer from financial difficulties. The literature revealed that in most single-mother households' economic mobility is lower than a two-parent household (Korkeila, Vahtera, Nabi, Kivimaki, Korkeila, Sumanen, and Koskenvuo, 2010; Popenoe, 1997; Sobolewski & Amato, 2005; Zhan, 2006). This is due to lower earning capacity, lack of available job opportunities, and few public benefits (Zhan, 2006). As a result, children reared in these homes are more likely to live in a poverty-ridden area. Accordingly, economic instability in a home has an indirect impact on a child, as it is known to erode the quality of the familial relationships; thus, this is also a factor which may explain depression in children (Sobolewski & Amato, 2005).

The research has demonstrated that single-parent families are less likely to engage in family activities than a two-parent family; have less emphasis on educational pursuits, and less access to social capital to assist in child rearing than a two-parent family, which are factors that may also explain childhood depression (Hollist & McBroom, 2006). Since protection and security are the primary components of an attachment relationship, children raised in a home lacking these elements may experience difficulty forming attachments to their caregivers (Bowlby, 1988). Children reared in a home with financial instability maybe less likely to have trust in their attachment figures' ability to protect and provide for their needs (Acock & Kiecolt, 1989). Also, may display less confidence and an inability to cope well with stress (Acock & Kiecolt, 1989). As a consequence, there was evidence that they maybe more susceptible to suffer from psychological difficulties, such as depression (Acock & Kiecolt, 1989). In contrast, children who were not raised in a lower socioeconomic bracket felt confident, secure, and trusted their attachment figures. These children were easily able to trust others and cope well with stressful situations; therefore, less likely to suffer from depression (Acock & Kiecolt, 1989).

Due to these facts, it is quite plausible that African-American men raised in a single-parent home without a biological father have a higher propensity to suffer from depression than men raised in a two-parent home with a father. Boys are twice as likely to be reported by their caregiver to suffer from concentration, emotional, and behavior difficulties (Osborne & McLanahan, 2007). Moreover, adult men are less likely to report symptoms of depression than women; therefore, the symptoms often go unrecognized and if untreated the depression will persist (FIFCFS, 2011).Currently, there is no research that explores whether there is a greater propensity for depression for adult African-American men who were reared in a home with limited or no paternal presence in the household.

Summary of Literature on Attachment and Depression

Insecurely attached individuals have traditionally been known to have a higher probability of suffering from depression. Researchers have explored possible reasons why insecure attachment is related to depression and some theorists believe that ineffective coping skills, and irregular care giving practices, and unavailable attachment figures can cause one to become hyper focused on emotion in order to gain attention from others. Some have argued that people who retain insecure attachment patterns do so because they have developed a negative view of themselves, based on an attachment figure's lack of response to their emotional needs. Additionally, it has been posed that insecure attachment was also correlated to depression due to negative self-view and negative view of others; namely, the belief that the self is not worthy of support from others and the belief that others will not be responsive to their needs. The overall implication of these theories was that internal working models are linked to a certain attachment classification and are associated to depression schemas, which may heighten a person's chance for developing depression. Overall, the literature review suggested that the theories surrounding links between attachment representation, views of self, and depression may be true. Thus far, there are only minimal studies which have investigated links between attachment and depression.

In order to conduct a research study, it is necessary to have a sound research method. The next chapter will delve into the research design and approach. It will provide information with regard to how the design derived logically from the problem statement. Moreover, this chapter will include a thorough description of the setting, sample, sampling method, sample size, and eligibility criteria for participants in the study. There will be an explanation of the materials and instruments used as well as a detailed description of the data. Finally, the data analysis will also be described and discussed.

Chapter 3: Research Method

Introduction

The goal of this research was to determine if there was a correlation between depression and attachment difficulties in adulthood after being raised in a single-parent home without a biological father figure. The first independent variable, paternal attachment, was defined as the desire to be in close proximity or in contact with one's paternal figure particularly in times of fear (Bowlby, 1982). Paternal attachment had four

levels: avoidant, secure, and ambivalent worry and ambivalent merger. Ambivalent worry

and merger are scales utilized in Carver's Measure of Attachment Qualities survey and

are similar to the insecure-resistant/anxious-ambivalent attachment classification, which

was discussed earlier in chapter 2. The second independent variable was the years of

paternal presence in the household during childhood. Paternal presence in the household

had three levels, (a) less than one year, (b) one to-six years, and (c) seven to twelve years.

The dependent variable was depression symptoms, which was characterized by "low

mood, pessimism, self-criticism, and retardation or agitation" (Beck, 1967, p. 10).

This chapter will introduce the research methods that were utilized to complete

this study. It will also present a detailed description of the research design methods,

research sampling process, research setting, procedures, data collection and analysis

practices, any threats to statistical conclusions and validity, and the procedures to ensure

participants safety. Lastly, for a brief review of this chapter a summary of its contents

will also be included.

Research Design and Approach

For the purpose of this research, a quantitative approach was chosen to assist with

determining whether there was a correlation between being raised in a single parent,

mother headed household with limited or no paternal presence and depression

propensities. Due to the fact that I did not manipulate any variables and there were no

interventions or treatments provided, a non-experimental design approach was chosen for this study, as opposed to an experimental design. There were no foreseeable time or resource issues associated with this design plan.

An analysis of variance (ANOVA) was chosen for this study to assist with measuring the mean difference in depression by duration of paternal absence during childhood. Likewise, this design was chosen to ascertain whether there was a mean difference between levels of attachment (secure, avoidant, and ambivalence worry/merger) and depression symptoms.

Methodology

Setting and Sample

The targeted population for this research was English speaking, African-American men between the ages of 18 to 55 who resided in Colorado located in the United States. In 2011, the African-American community included approximately 42 million people and reported to be the second largest minority group in the United States (U.S. Census, 2012). The United States Census Bureau (2012) defined African-American as "a person who has any origins in any of the Black racial groups of Africa" (2). The participants were individuals raised in a single-parent home headed by a mother with limited or no biological paternal presence. In order to understand the research packet information, the participants were required to at minimum read at a 6th grade level. I selected the participants from a health fair held in Colorado. The health fair was a public forum; therefore, I did not need permission to conduct the study at this location. The number of participants that I utilized in this study was 92. I provided all the participants with a written statement prior to data collection informing them that their participation in this study is strictly voluntary.

Sample size. I conducted a power analysis, using GPower3 software to determine the appropriate sample size for the study. An apriori power analysis, assuming a medium effect size (f = .40), a = .05, indicated a minimum sample size of 92 participants was required to achieve a power of .80. Please see the below, Figure 1, for an example of the power analysis that I conducted to assist in determining the appropriate sample size for this study.

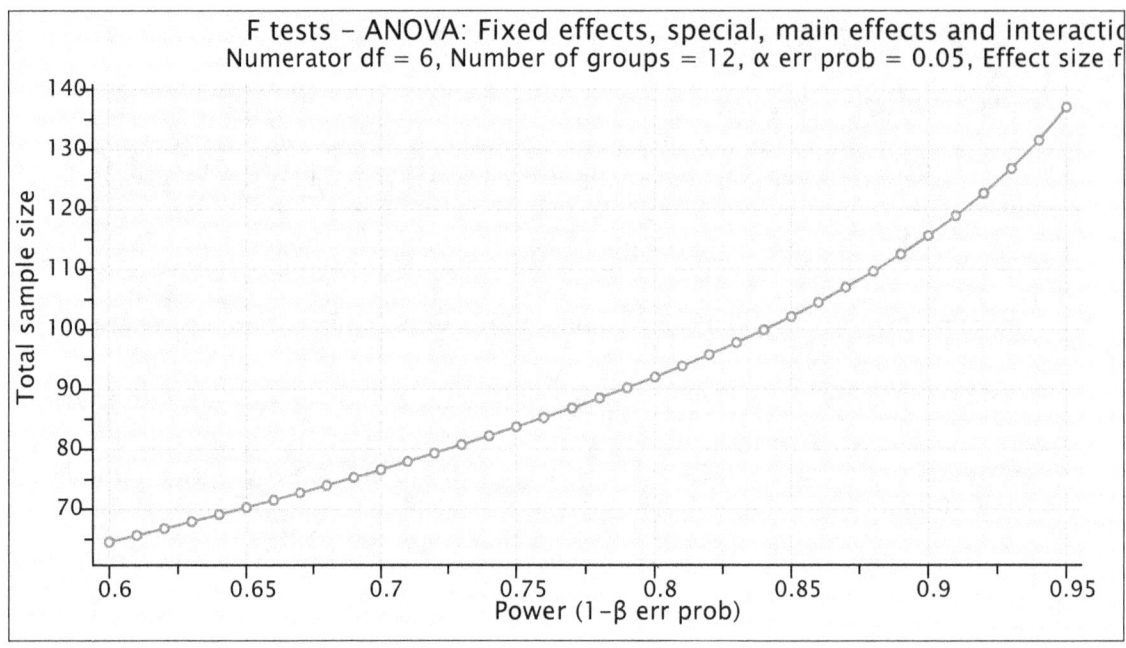

Figure 1. Power as a function of sample size.

The use of a medium effect size (f = .40) was appropriate for this proposed research study. In a study conducted by Kamkar, Doyle, and Markiewicz (2012), designed to measure whether insecure attachments to parents resulted in early adolescence depression, calculated an effect size of .40. Ruijten, Roelofs, and Rood (2011) conducted a study focusing on rumination and quality of attachment to parents and depression in adolescence and found an effect size at .41 (p < .01). The aforementioned studies yielded an average effect size of .29 (p < .01); therefore, I determined that an average effect size for this study would be .40 (medium).

Sampling procedures. Sampling is an important component for any study, as it can provide a quick and easy method to study a sample of the population rather than a whole population (Shao, 1999). The primary objective of sampling methods is to assist the researcher in selecting the population that will be included in the sample (Shao, 1999). Accordingly, there are two groups of sampling methods utilized in research: probability sampling and non-probability sampling (Shao, 1999). Probability sampling utilizes random selection to assist the researcher in sampling the population (Shao, 1999). In contrast, non-probability sampling methods allow the researcher to use their judgment when sampling the population. Normally, with this type of sampling method the researcher will combine theory, experience, and knowledge of the research when sampling the population (Shao, 1999). Non-probability sampling methods include: quota sampling, purposive, sampling, convenience sampling, snowball sampling, and self-section sampling (Shao, 1999). For the purpose of this study, I have chosen to utilize a convenience sampling technique, a non-probability sampling strategy.

For this study a convenience sampling technique was determined to be appropriate. Convenience sampling is a common sampling strategy among researchers, as it allows the researcher an easy and quick way to sample a large population (Shao, 1999). This sampling strategy was chosen because it will allow me the opportunity to sample the participants that are readily available at the health convention. I will recruit participations who are at the convention and who hear about the study through associates.

Inclusions and exclusions. African-American men were included in this sample. However, African-American men who did not fit the population criteria were not included in this study. Likewise, for the purposes of this research, no Caucasian men or females were included in this sample.

Data Collection and Analysis

Data Collection

In effort to facilitate this research, self-report questionnaires were utilized. Self-report surveys are widely used in research, as McDonald (2008) reported that over 95% of the studies presented in the *Journal of Personality* utilized self-report measures. There are many advantages for utilizing self-report measures in one's research. For instance, when wanting to learn intimate information about someone it is most advantageous to go directly to the person. Gathering information directly from the source, allows one not only to get the most information about one's source, but also to get accurate information (McDonald, 2008). Furthermore, self-report measures are time-saving tools, as they are relatively easy to interpret. Lastly, self-report measures are relatively inexpensive, which also lends to their popularity (McDonald, 2008). However, there are some disadvantages to utilizing self-report measures in research. For example, self-report measures are imperfect, as the questions may be easily misinterpreted causing incorrect results to be obtained (McDonald, 2008). Likewise, self-report surveys have the potential for response bias, as individuals may attempt to present themselves in a positive light or over report their symptoms, which could create incorrect results (McDonald, 2008).

Procedures. On September 1st and September 7th, I went in person to a free, public health fair, which was held in a suburban location in Colorado and recruited participants for my study. This was accomplished by putting together a research packet, which included a cover letter, a demographic self-report survey, the Measure of Attachment Qualities assessment, and the Beck Depression Inventory-II assessment and distributing the packets at the health fair. While at the health fair, I approached participants who appeared to fit my study criteria and explained my research and asked them if they would like to participate. Once approval had been granted, I directed the participants to a private location and handed the research packet to them. The participants were allowed time to read the cover letter (see Appendix A for review of this form) and the informed consent (see Appendix B for review of this form). They were informed that they could complete the packet at the health fair or they could mail the packet to me in the self-addressed stamped envelope that I would provide them. Furthermore, I directed the participants to not include any information that may identify them on any of the forms, as permission will be granted by returning the surveys. This step is necessary to insure that the participants remain anonymous so as to maintain the integrity of the research process. Lastly, the cover letter provided the participants with my direct information in case they had any questions while completing the study or after the study had been finished.

Once the informed consent was granted and the cover letter had been read, the participants were verbally directed by me to complete the assessments included in the research packet or return them on a later date in the self-addressed stamped envelope. A lock box was placed beside me for the participants who wished to complete the surveys at the health fair. Upon completion of the surveys, those participants were directed to fold the packet and place it into the lock box. Once the surveys had been returned, they were reminded by me that my contact information was included on the cover letter for follow-up information regarding the study. I did not debrief the participants after the data had been gathered.

I collected the demographic information (see Appendix C to review this form) from the demographic survey, which was included in the research packet. The demographic information that was gathered from the included: age, education level, and marital status. Once all the data had been collected and placed in the lock box and the participants had been provided my contact information; I took the lock box and placed it in a locked closet located in my home office.

Instrumentation and Materials

The Beck Depression Inventory-Second Edition (BDI-II) is a self-report measure, which was designed in 1996 by Aaron T. Beck, Robert A. Steer, and Gregory K. Brown to detect depression symptoms in adolescents and adults. The BDI-II contains 21 items and each includes a list of four statements, which are organized in levels of severity of depression symptoms. The majority of the items are measured on a 4-point Likert scale, which vary from 0 to 3. In order to access differences in behavior and motivation, many of the response items have seven response options. In order to score the BDI-II, one will need to add the ratings for the 21 items. The highest total number one can obtain is 63.

In order to test the reliability of the BDI-II, Beck, Brown, and Steer (1996) conducted a study, which utilized 500 psychiatric outpatients. This study reported a coefficient alpha of .92. Beck et al. (1996) conducted a second study, which included 120 college students, which yielded a coefficient alpha of .93. It is important to note that both studies' coefficient alphas showed a marked improvement from the previous versions of the BDI.

In effort to assess the BDI-II's validity, Beck et al. (1996) reported the following correlations with existing measures: Beck Scale for Suicide Ideation (BSS) $r = .37$, $n = 158$; Beck Hopelessness Scale (BHS) $r = .68$, $n = 158$; Hamilton Psychiatric Rating Scale for Depression (HPRSD) $r = .71$, $n = 87$; and the Hamilton Rating Scale for anxiety (HRSA) $r = 47$, $n = 87$ (Beck et al., 1996). These results show good construct validity; therefore, it would be an appropriate tool to utilize for this study.

Additionally, the Measurement of Attachment Qualities (MAQ) was utilized to ascertain the following attachment styles: secure, avoidant, ambivalent worry, and ambivalent merger. The MAQ is a self-report questionnaire and was determined to be more appropriate for this survey study as opposed to the Adult Attachment Interview (AAI), which was designed in an interview format. The MAQ consists of 14 questions answered on a 4-point Likert scale (*disagree a lot, disagree a little, agree a little,* and, *agree a lot* = 4). In order to categorize attachment, responses for each subscale were added. Four of the response items focused on the avoidant attachment pattern, three items assessed the secure attachment pattern and the last seven items evaluated two categorical patterns of ambivalent attachment. Lastly, I determined the predominant attachment style from the highest average score obtained between the two scales.

Carver (1997) tested the reliability of the MAQ with a study of 807 undergraduate students: 355 men and 452 females. The test-retest reliability was as follows: (a) avoidance test-retest was r = .80, (b) secure test-retest was $r = .61$, (c) ambivalent-worry test-retest was $r = .69$, and (d) ambivalent-merger $r = .69$. Validity of the MAQ strong correlations with related questionnaires: the Relationship Questionnaire (Bartholomew & Horowitz, 1991) and an additional assessment, which was developed by Hazan and Shaver (1987). Thus, the MAQ's has good construct validity and reliability; therefore, would be an appropriate tool to utilize for this study. On the MAQ website, the creator, Carver (1997) has granted permission to utilize this tool for research (For copyright statement see Appendix C).

A demographic survey was designed by me and included 7 response items (See Appendix A for the complete survey). I included a question in the survey in order to assess the number of years the biological father was present in the participant's life. The question asked: *During your childhood and adolescence years, how many years were you in the home with your biological father?* There were three response items included in this survey: no biological father presence in the home (less than one year), biological father present (one to six years), and biological father present (seven to twelve years). This survey was included in the research packet and was stapled to the Beck Depression Scale Inventory-II and the Measure of Attachment Qualities assessment.

Data Analysis

Analysis

I chose to utilize an Analysis of Variance (ANOVA) with an $\alpha = .05$ to assist me in comparing the depression means as opposed to several different t-tests analysis in effort to respond to the research questions associated with this study. An ANOVA is a statistical analysis utilized when there are two groups or more, as it will measure the variance between and within those groups. I did not choose to utilize a t-test for this study, as it only measures a significant difference between two groups. T-tests would not be sufficient to measure means between multiple groups, because one would have to run several t-tests to analysis multiple hypotheses at one time, which would not control for the type one error (Mitchell & Jolley, 2004). A type one error can occur when the null hypothesis is falsely rejected when it is actually true (Mitchell & Jolley, 2004).

The research results were expected to reveal evidence that participants with insecure attachment styles would have a higher level of depression symptoms in comparison to participants with secure attachment styles. Likewise, I expected the results to reveal evidence that participants with no paternal presence in the home or low paternal presence would have higher levels of depression symptoms than participants who had medium paternal presence in the home. Finally, it was hypothesized that the participants attachment style would be associated with the number of years of paternal presence.

In order to conduct an ANOVA, I utilized the SPSS 21.0 Graduate Pack Statistical software to obtain all data. This software was purchased, licensed, and downloaded by me on my personal laptop..

Research Questions

1. Is there an association between attachment and depression, in African-American men between the ages of 18 to 55 years?

2. Is there an association between parental presence and depression, in African-American men between the ages of 18 to 55 years?

3. Is the effect of paternal presence on depression different for secure versus avoidant attachment?

Hypotheses

1. Null Hypothesis (H_0): There will be no significant main effect of paternal attachment on depression.

   Alternative Hypothesis (H_1): There will be a significant main effect of paternal attachment on depression.

2. Null Hypothesis (H_0): There will be no significant main effect of parental presence on depression.

   Alternative Hypothesis (H_1): There will be a significant main effect of parental presence on depression.

3. Null Hypothesis (H_0): There will be no attachment by paternal presence interaction effect on depression,

   Alternative Hypothesis (H_1): There will be an attachment by paternal presence interaction on depression.

Threats to Validity

Conclusion Validity

Threats to conclusion validity can occur when the researcher wrongly rejects the null hypothesis when; in fact, it is correct. These conditions can include the following, but are not limited to these areas: (a) sample size, (b) reliability of the instrument, and (c) data assumptions. I conducted an a priori power analysis to ensure that the appropriate sample size will be chosen. Also, the reliability of the instruments that were utilized for this study appear to be excellent.

External Validity

Threats to external validity are important to consider when conducting research as they, too, can cause me to wrongly reject the null hypothesis. Some threats to external validity include, but are not limited to the following: (a) can the results be generalized to other populations, and (b) can the results be generalized to other environmental settings. Since the participants in this study were African-American men, the study results cannot be generalized to other populations. Likewise, the convenience sampling method and recruitment methods may have introduced bias.

Internal Validity

When conducting research a concern for threats to internal validity should be considered by me. Such threats to internal validity include but are not limited to the following: (a) determining the cause-effect relationship of study, and (b) establishing that an event caused or influenced or changed the behavior. From this retrospective study, no conclusions can be drawn on cause and effect.

Data Assumptions

The statistical test that was utilized to answer the research questions was a two-way ANOVA analysis. There are some important assumptions of ANOVA. The first assumption is normality of the dependent variable. Brandimarte (2011) explained that there are two primary ways to test for normality, i.e. statistical testing or through visual examination. He further expounded that because statistical testing allows for objectivity it has an advantage over visual examination; however, in the event of small samples or very large samples this method may be overly or under sensitive. Brandimarte (2011) further added that a visual examination through plots and graphs is the preferred method to test for normality. I chose to use visual examination through the use of a Q-Q plot and histogram. A Q-Q plot and histogram were useful to ascertain the degree in which the measured variable fell within the normal distribution range. It is believed that this method allows me a subjective means to test for normality without sensitivity problems.

Homogeneity of variance between groups is also another assumption of the ANOVA. It has been found that homogeneity of variance can happen in research if there is the same amount of participants in the groups. I assessed this through the use of Levene's Test for Equality of Variance.

Protection of Data

When conducting research, it is important to protect the data in order to ensure the integrity of the research. This was accomplished by insuring that each participant did not leave any identifying information on the research packets. Additionally, each participant was instructed upon completion of the surveys to place the research packet in a locked box. Once all research packets had been retrieved the lock box was placed in my locked closet located in the home office.

Upon collection of data, it was transferred into an electric format in order to create an electric file. I saved the file onto the hard drive on my laptop and on a flash drive. Both files on the laptop and the flash drive were secured, as they were password protected and I was the only one with access to the passwords. Furthermore, I stored the flash drive in the lock box when it was not in use.

Protection of Participants

With any research it is necessary to ensure the protection of the participants to ensure that they are not harmed during the research process. The American Psychological Association Code 1.11 requires that I obtain agreement from the participant prior to conducting the research. I notified the participants that agreement was implied by return of the completed survey. Likewise, I informed each participant that they were not required to participate in this research, as their participation was strictly voluntary. Additionally, the participants were informed that they were allowed to end their participation in this study at any time without any negative consequences. In further effort to ensure the participant's safety, I selected a safe location to conduct the study.

Summary

I explored in this study whether there was a correlation between attachment and depression symptoms for adult African-American men who were raised in a single parent household by a mother with limited or no biological paternal figure. I conducted a nonexperimental, quantitative, survey study, which included 92 participants. The data was collected and gathered from a health fair held in Colorado. Chapter 4 will discuss the findings.

Chapter 4: Results

Introduction

The purpose of this nonexperimental, quantitative study was to examine whether there was a correlation between attachment styles (avoidant, secure, and ambivalent worry/merger) and biological paternal presence (less than one year, one to six years, and seven to twelve years). The first independent variable, paternal attachment, was defined as the desire to be in close proximity or in contact with one's paternal figure particularly in times of fear (Bowlby, 1982). The second independent variable was the years of paternal presence in the household. The dependent variable was depression symptoms, which as characterized by "low mood, pessimism, self-criticism, and retardation or agitation" (Beck, 1967, p. 10). This chapter will review descriptive statistics, evaluate statistical assumptions in correlation with a factorial analysis of variance. Likewise, this chapter will examine the reliability of the Measures of Attachment Qualities measurement and examine the study's results obtained from a 2x3 factor analysis of variance.

Descriptive Statistics

Sampling method: For the purpose of this research, I used a convenience sampling method to recruit 92 African-American men between the ages of 18-55 from Denver, Colorado. African-Americans make up approximately 4.3% of the population in Colorado (U.S. Census, 2013). A total of 116 research packets were distributed by me and 92 packets were returned. See Table 3 for a summary of the study demographics.

Table 3

Demographics Characteristics of Study Sample (N=92)

Characteristic	n	%	
	Age		
18-23	14	15.2	
24-29	15	16.3	
30-35	15	16.3	
36-41	18	19.6	
42-47	17	18.5	
48-55	13	14.1	
Total	92	100.0	
	Marital Status		%
Divorced	9		9.8
Married	24		26.1
Separated	3		3.3
Single	56		60.9
Total	92		100.0
	Education Level		%
Associates Degree	15		16.3
Bachelor's Degree	23		25.0
GED	15		16.3
High School	30		32.6
Master's Degree	9		9.8
Total	92		100.0

Evaluation of Assumptions

With a two-way ANOVA analysis, there are some important assumptions that one should explore. The first is of normality within the dependent variables. Homogeneity of variance between groups is also another assumption of the ANOVA. It has been found that homogeneity of variance can happen in research if there is the same amount of participants in the groups. Additionally, the presence of outliers can have a negative impact on the research data set; therefore, negatively impacting the validity of the research.

Normality

A Kolmogorov-Smirnov analysis was conducted in order to assess whether normality was distributed within the dependent variables. This analysis yielded a significant *p*-value of .013. A normal distribution of the dependent variable is considered significant above .05; thus, the assumption of normality has been met. In effort to further determine that this assumption has been met, a histogram and a Q-Q plot was generated in order to provide a visual depiction.

Normality can be determined by the use of a histogram. One can assess normality by visually inspecting the histogram and determining whether a perfect bell shape is present. After a visual inspection of the histogram (Figure 2) generated for this study, it was determined that a perfect bell shape was not evident. However, this is not unusual due to the fact that only a small number of the population was assessed. Schmider, Ziegler, Danay, Beyer, and Buhner (2010) analyzed 400 studies which presented violations of the assumption of normally distributed data and determined that ANOVA was robust under this situation. Additionally, another important factor when determining normality is to determine whether outliers are present. The histogram revealed that there were no outliers present. Due to the above reasons, it has been determined that normality of the dependent variable has been met. Similar to the histogram, the Q-Q plot (Figure 3) revealed no outliers present and demonstrated a relatively straight line; therefore, it has been concluded that normality has been met.

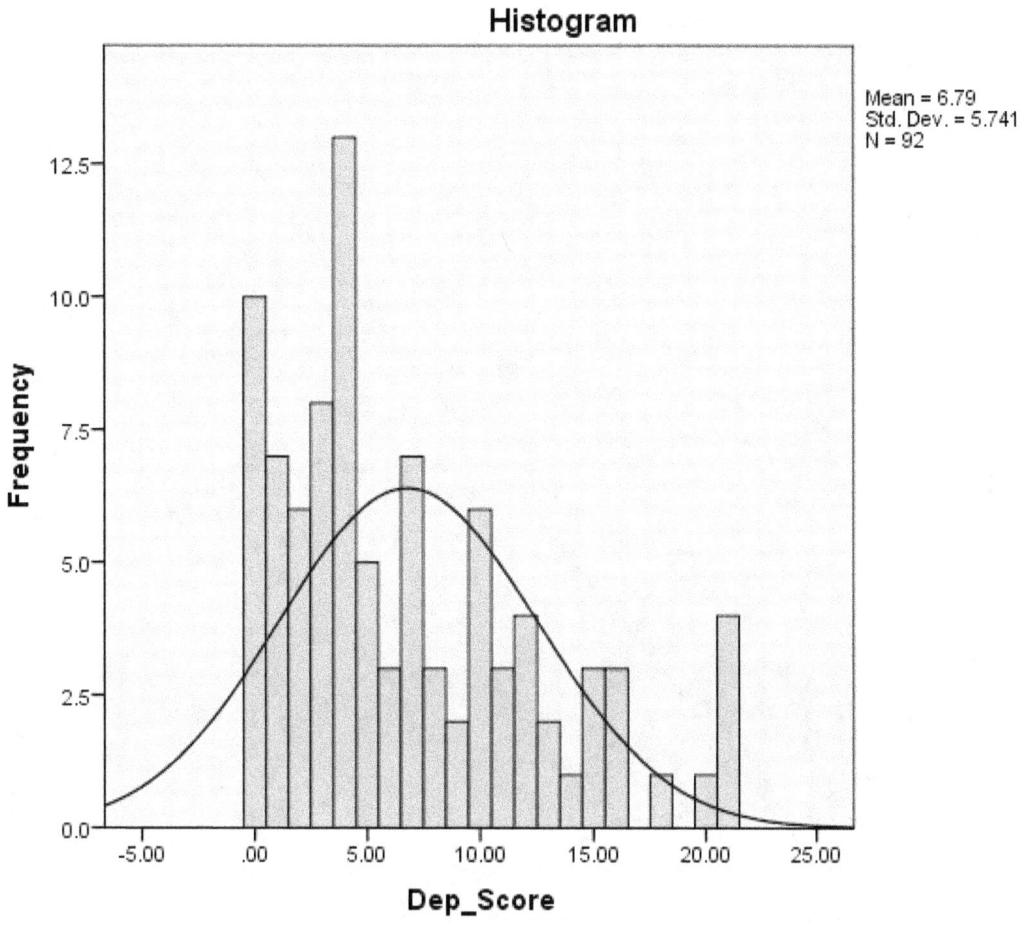

Figure 2. Histogram of frequency of depression scores.

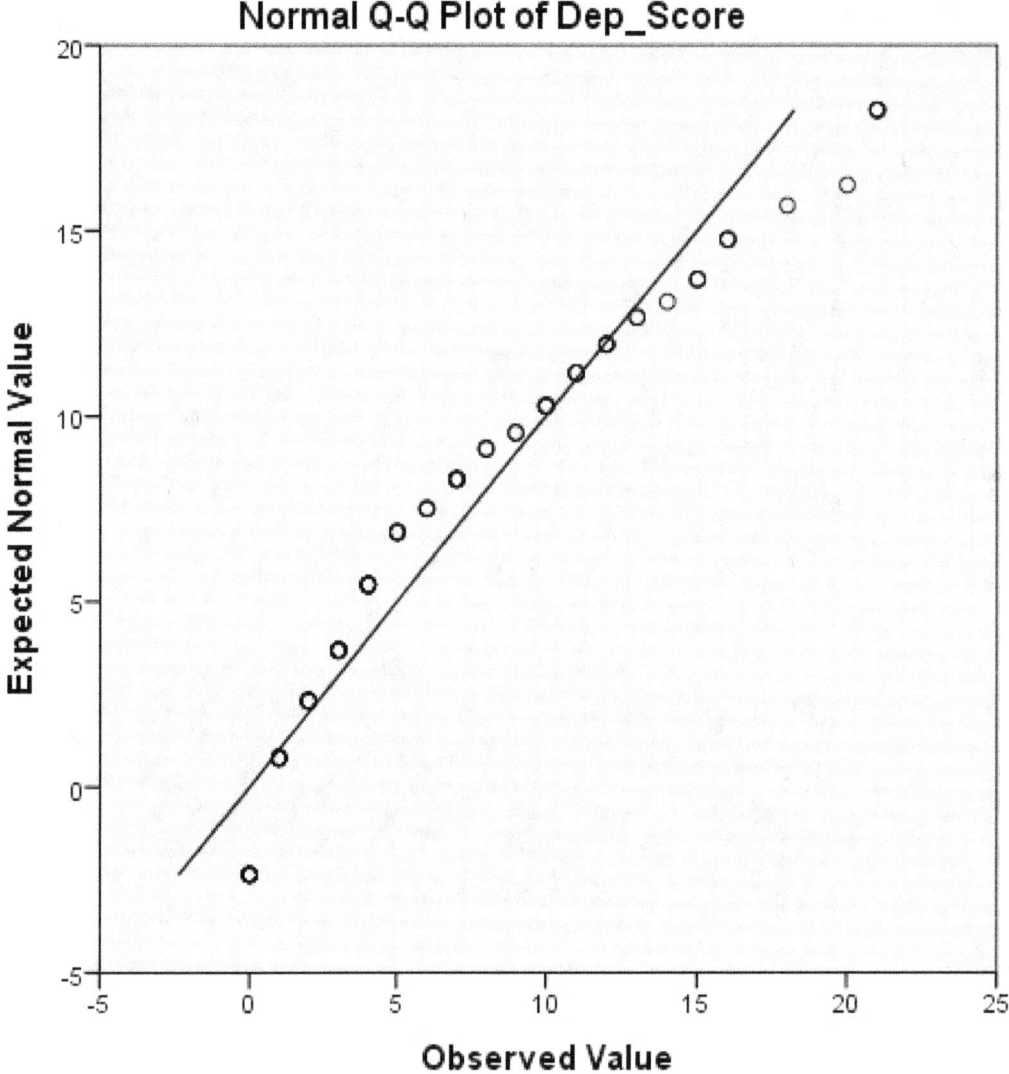

Figure 3. Q-Q plot.

Homogeneity of Variance

In order to test for equality of variance between groups, a Levene's Test of Variance was conducted. This analysis yielded a non-significant value ($F=.337$, $P=.563$), which is higher than .05; therefore, equality of variance was met.

Outliers

Outliers can have an adverse impact on a study's data set. In order to look for

outliers in this studies' data set, a descriptive analysis was utilized to assess the mean

score and trim mean score at 5%. The descriptive analysis yielded a mean score of 6.80

and a 6.40 trimmed mean score. The mean score and trimmed mean score are almost

within range of each other, which indicates that there are no extreme scores present in the

data set. Likewise, in effort to further determine whether there were any outliers present a

box plot (see Figure 4) was also generated. The box plot results also revealed that there

were no outliers present.

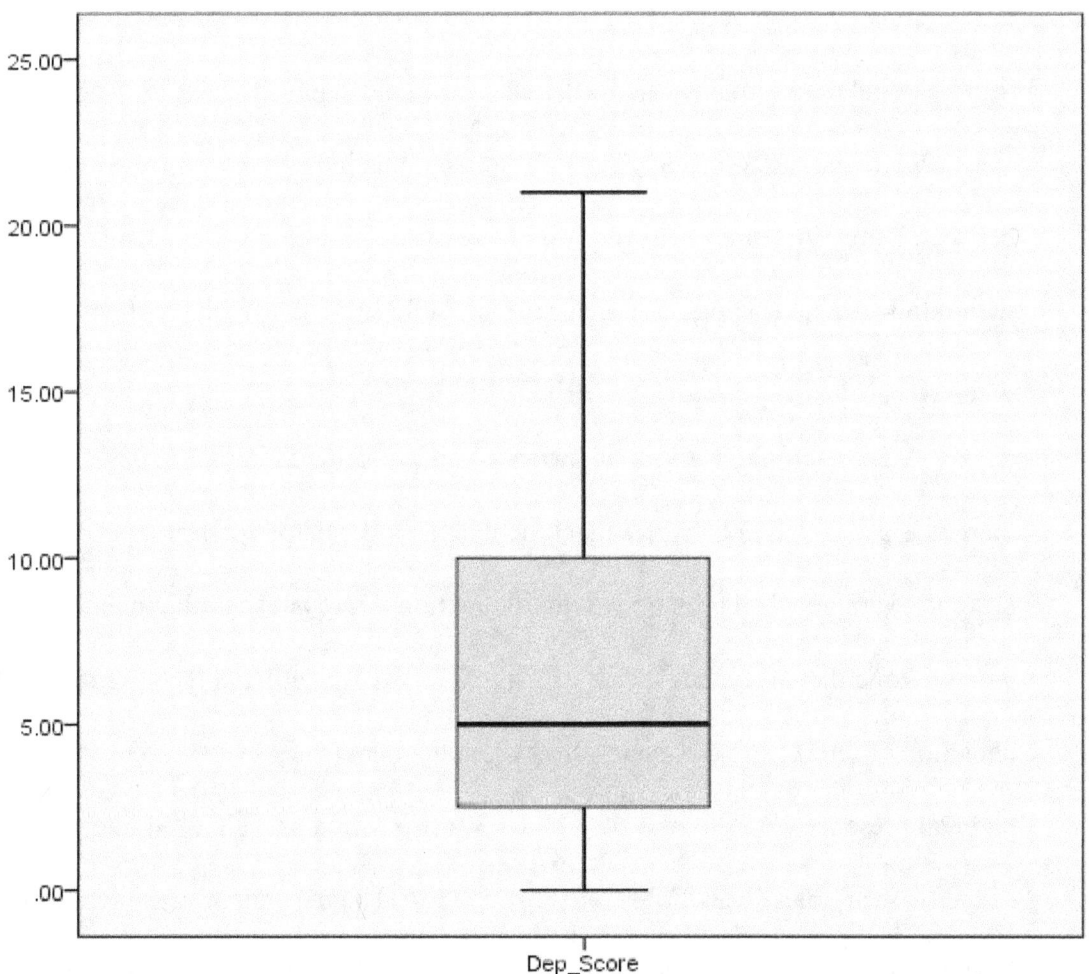

Figure 4. Box plot of dependent variable, depression.

Reliability Analysis

In effort to determine whether BDI-II and MAQ were appropriate assessment tools to utilize for this study's population, I used the Cronbach's alpha coefficient. Because Cronbach's alpha only requires the user to administer one test, unlike other measures (test-retest), it has become a popular means to measure reliability. The results for the MAQ were the following: avoidance =.35, secure =.27, ambivalent (worry) = .06, and ambivalent (merger) = .22. Although the MAQ has been found to be a reliable tool as mentioned in chapter 3, these scores indicate that the MAQ was not an appropriate tool for this population. Finally, the BDI-II scored a coefficient alpha =.44. Accordingly, de Vaus (2002) suggested that any score less than .30 is indicative of a weak correlation between items. A score of .70 would have revealed high internal consistency reliability within this sample. Chapter 5 will discuss possible reasons why this did not occur.

Inferential Statistics

A 2x3 factorial analysis of variance was performed in order to assess whether there was a correlation between attachment style and paternal presence. Additionally, in order to examine whether there was an interaction effect between the independent variables and the dependent variable a 2x3 ANOVA was utilized (see Figure 5 for depiction of interaction). A main effect of attachment ($F(1, 86) = 4.153, p = .045$) and parental presence ($F(2, 86) = 3.665, p = .030$) was found as well as an interaction effect of the two variables ($F(2, 86)) = 3.818, p = .026$). The dependent variables explained 0.045% of depression scores. The full 2x3 ANOVA results are depicted below in Table 6.

Although there were four attachment styles, the participants scored the lowest in the

ambivalent scales (worry/merger). Out of the 92 participants, 83 scored high in the

avoidant scale.

Table 4

Frequency of Attachment

		Frequency	Percent	Valid Percent	Cumulative Percent
Valid	Secure Attachment	9	9.8	9.8	9.8
	Avoidant Attachment	83	90.2	90.2	100.0
	Total	92	100.0	100.0	

Table 5

Frequency of Paternal Presence

		Frequency	Percent	Valid Percent	Cumulative Percent
Valid	Less than 1 year	32	34.8	34.8	34.8
	1 to 6 years	31	33.7	33.7	68.5
	7 to 12 years	29	31.5	31.5	100.0
	Total	92	100.0	100.0	

Table 6

ANOVA Results: - Dependent Variable: Dependent Variable Depression

Source	Type III Sum of Squares	df	Mean Square	F	Sig.
Corrected Model	.866a	5	.173	1.851	.112
Intercept	1.137	1	1.137	12.148	.001
Attachment	.389	1	.389	4.153	.045
Paternal	.686	2	.343	3.665	.030
Attachment * Paternal	.714	2	.357	3.818	.026
Error	8.047	86	.094		
Total	10.000	92			
Corrected Total	8.913	91			

Note. R Squared = .097 (Adjusted R Squared = .045)

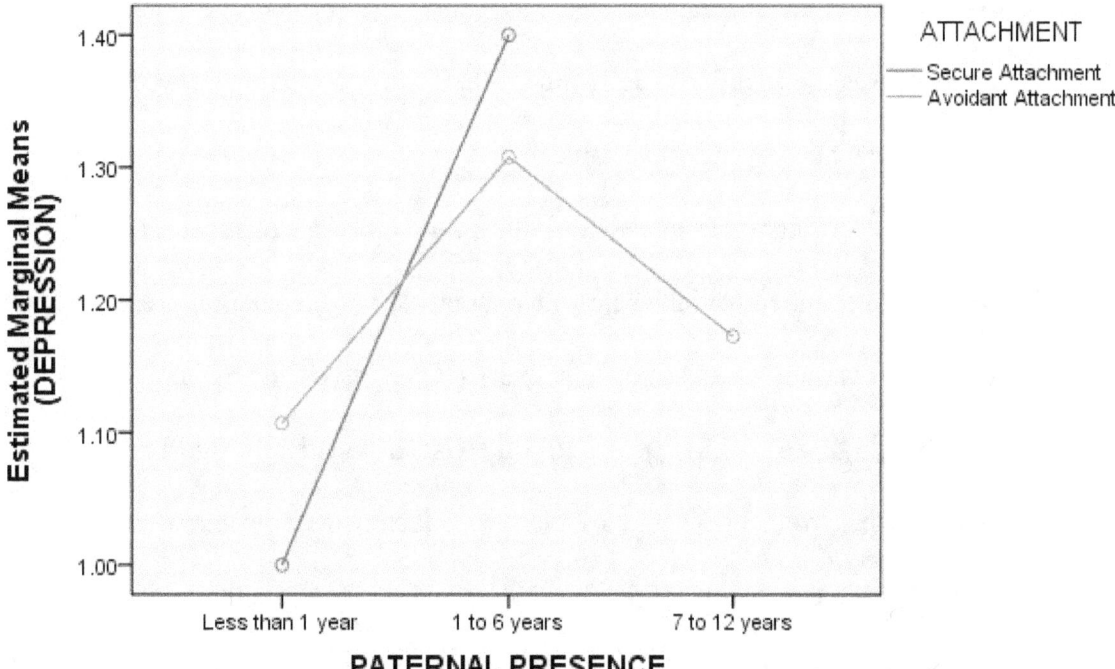

Figure 5. Estimated means of depression (x axis - attachment and y axis - paternal presence)

Summary

The purpose of this nonexperimental, quantitative study was to examine the interrelationship between African-American men's paternal attachment and depression propensities. Moreover, this research set out to determine if this relationship is mediated by years of paternal presence (limited or no presence). Based on the study criteria, all the participants were African-American men between the ages of 18-55, who were raised in a single-parent home with limited or no biological paternal presence. The demographics revealed that 60.9% of the participants have never been married and 51.1% of the participants were college graduates. All participants resided in Colorado. A statistical analysis was run in order to determine if there was correlation between the studies independent and dependent variables.

According to the statistical findings, there was a statistical relationship between the two independent variables i.e., attachment styles and paternal presence with the dependent variable depression. The 2x3 ANOVA revealed an interaction between the variables, $F(2, 86) = 3.818$, $p = .026$. Likewise, a statistically significant presence between the two independent variables i.e., attachment and paternal presence was also found. The between-subjects analysis of variance revealed a main effect of attachment and paternal presence, $F(1, 86) = 4.153$, $p = .045$ and $F(2, 86) = 3.665$, $p = .030$, respectively.

The results above indicate that there was an interaction between the study variables. These findings suggest that the lack of a biological paternal figure in the home may adversely impact African-American men. Additionally, these results suggest that attachment difficulties in adulthood may also be a concern for these men. This next chapter will provide a detailed summary of these key study's findings. It will also present the limitations of the study and how the findings relate to past and current literature. The research methodology will be explained as well as the theoretical implications of the study. Next, the social change implications of this research will also be discussed along with recommendations for future studies. Although there were four attachment styles, none of the participants scored in the ambivalent scales (worry/merger). Out of the 92 participants, 83 scored in the avoidant range. This high score in the avoidant range may be related to the small sampling pool that was utilized for this research. Additionally, 61% of the participants in this study were single, which can also account for the high score in the avoidant range.

Chapter 5: Discussion, Conclusions, and Recommendations

Introduction

The study's hypothesis was that the independent variables (attachment and paternal presence) would significantly predict depression propensities for the study sample. This chapter will provide a brief interpretation and summary of the study's findings. Next, a discussion of the social change implications, recommendations for future research, and suggestions for future research will be detailed.

Interpretation of the Findings

The study's result revealed a slight association between attachment styles and paternal presence on the study's participants' depression propensities. Likewise, the main effects for attachment style and paternal presence were found to have had a significant interaction (see the Inferential Statistics section in chapter 4). These findings suggest that there is a correlation between being raised in a single-parent home without a biological father and suffering from attachment and depression in adulthood. The results of this study were not surprising, as Amato (1991) conducted a study which discovered a significant interaction between parental absence and race/ethnicity at $p < .04$. These results revealed that African-Americans were the most negatively impacted by the absence of a parent than other ethnic/racial groups. This research was similar to my study because both were able to identify that African-Americans may be significantly impacted by paternal absence. Amato (1991) was unable to identify a link between gender and paternal absence; however, my study was able to identify a correlation between African-American men and paternal absence.

Likewise, Chapter 2 discussed Bowlby's (1973) attachment theory in which he theorized that the need to be in close proximity to a primary attachment figure was an instinctual need that dated back to early humans. Ainsworth (1978) agreed with Bowlby, but took his theory a step farther and explained that the relationship between primary attachment figures and children was a dyadic one which involved affective communication between both parties. The current findings of this study proves the importance of Bowlby's and Ainsworth's theories, as it was able to demonstrate that there is a correlation between absent primary attachment figures and depression. Other literature was found to be in alignment with this study's results too, as it has been theorized that rejection by a primary attachment figure during childhood has been equated with depressive symptoms, as the child may internalize this perceived rejection to be their fault and consequently develop negative self-view of themselves and the world around them (Oliver, 2003).

Limitations of the Study

This study yielded several limitations, which may have impacted the study results. The first limitation of this study was that the target population consisted of African-American men in Colorado, with the majority of subjects being of college age and unmarried. As a result, the study results may not be generalizable to the male African-American population at large. The low Cronbach's alpha did not reveal a high internal consistency score and may indicate that this measurement was not a good fit for the participant pool. This study also did not have a high internal consistency, unlike a previous study conducted by Carver (1997). The exact reasons for this discrepancy have not been confirmed, but are likely due in part to differences in the sample sets. For example, this study solely consisted of African-American men; whereas Carver's (1997) study utilized mixed-race subjects of both genders. The discrepancy suggests that the impact of paternal absence differs based on family demographics.

An additional limitation of this study was that it centered on African-American men who were raised with limited or no biological paternal presence. I failed to include in the study African-American men who were raised biological paternal presence and it failed to consider African-American men who were raised with stepfathers. This means that absence of a biological father may have been negated by presence of other male attachment figures and our observed effects may be underestimating the real effect size. On the other hand, being raised in a single-parent household often is associated with economic disadvantage which increases the risk of depressive symptoms; thus, our effect sizes may be smaller than observed. Future studies are needed to examine the association between parental absence and depression in more depth taking into account some of these variables. Additionally, the use of self-report measures to gather data presents a limitation as well, as I did not consider that participants may not be truthful about their symptoms.

Finally, there was an unequal distribution among the attachment styles and a low endorsement of certain attachment styles. It is recommended that future research in this area utilize a larger sample and more varied attachment styles, before any conclusions can be drawn regarding the interaction between attachment styles and depression.

Reliability of Instrumentation

In effort to assess whether the correct instruments were used to gather data from the population in this study, their reliability was measured. The Cronbach's Alpha was utilized to assess the reliability of the Beck Depression Scale and the Measures of Attachment Qualities scale. Internal reliability was low (ranging from 0.21 to 0.44). These scores indicated that the above tools were not reliable measures to utilize for the population of participants in this study. As mentioned previously, the validity of the BDI-II and the MAQ were examined and both were deemed to be reliable tools, as the MAQ yielded alpha .69 and the BDI-II yielded alpha of .92. Tavakol and Dennick (2011) discuss that it is not unusual to yield different alpha results for the same measure, because alpha is a product of the participants' scores. Accordingly, the alpha scores will vary with each study.

Recommendations for Action

Although the measurement tools were found not to be appropriate for the participants in this study, the study results concurred with the original hypothesis that attachment style (secure, avoidant, ambivalent worry, and ambivalent merger) and paternal presence (less than one year, one to six years, and and seven to twelve years) would predict depression propensities for the sample population. In order to ensure more accurate results relating to the research questions and hypothesis, future researchers should address all the limitations of this study. The first limitation that must be addressed by future researchers is to include other racial populations in their study in effort to have a more diverse population pool. Because this study was solely conducted in Colorado it may not be generalizable; therefore, it would be necessary for future researchers to include other geographic locations in their study. Thirdly, another limitation of this study was the narrowed age range; in order to avoid this limitation, it would be advantageous for future researchers to widen the age range. Likewise, this study failed to consider homes with stepfathers and this should be considered in future studies, as it can also impact study results. Finally, this study did not consider how being raised by a single mother may cause an economic disparity, which could also impact the study's result. By focusing on the aforementioned limitations, future researchers should be able to address the disparities of the participant pool.

Recommendations for Further Study

The literature review found no scholarly studies that set out to address how the lack of a biological paternal figure in the home may cause attachment and depression difficulties for adult African-American men. Past studies have failed to associate these variables and instead have focused attention on the number of African-American men in prison (Battle, S. F., 2002; Daniels, 1986; Wildeman, 2009). They failed to recognize or consider that attention to these men's home environment and its impact on their mental health may be required prior to imprisonment. Future research may shed light on this issue and may encourage therapeutic initiatives to be developed and implemented as a preventative measure to imprisonment. African-American children are significantly more likely to be raised in a father-absent home and are subject to suffer from mental health difficulties in adulthood; the social cost makes the study of this epidemic of high importance to society (United States Department of Labor Bureau of Labor Statistics, 2013). Although this study results determined that that there was an interaction between the study variables, there are limitations. One way to expand on this research would be to conduct a gender comparison study. Future researchers could investigate how these variables impact the different genders. Likewise, it may be beneficial for future researchers to conduct a comparison study among different ethnic groups in order to determine whether different results would be yielded.

Cronbach's Alpha was utilized to ascertain the reliability of the attachment and depression tools utilized for the participants in this study. Although these instruments were determined to be reliable measures for these constructs, they were found not to be appropriate tools for the participants in this study. It is believed that this discrepancy may be related to this study's small population. It is recommended that future studies in this area have a larger sampling pool. Additionally, this study's focus was on African-American males only and it is believed that this may have contributed to the tools not meeting the reliability standards. It is recommended that future studies include a more diverse population in order to meet reliability standards. Although the assessment tools were deemed not appropriate for this study's population, an interaction between attachment and depression was evident.

This study's findings were similar to other studies' results, as other researchers have hypothesized that the absence of a primary attachment figure would have adverse impact on that child (Burns, 2008; Mercer, 2006; Prior, Glasser, & Kingsley, 2006). However, there was no research available that focused solely on how limited or no biological paternal presence during childhood impacted adult African-American men' attachment style and depression propensities. As mentioned previously, African-American children are at a higher risk than other ethnic groups to be raised in a home with limited or no biological paternal presence (U.S. Department of Labor Bureau of Labor Statistics, 2013). It is suggested from this research that continued study in this area would be beneficial in effort to assist in developing a better understanding of this pervasive syndrome.

Implications for Social Change

The major finding of this study is that paternal absence has a strong negative impact on African-American men. This finding underscores the importance of setting up community mentor programs and other initiatives to educate the importance of parental responsibility. The importance of these mechanisms for social change is underscored by the results of previous studies, that show the loss of a paternal figure during childhood often serves as a precursor to children developing negative self-schema, frequently leading to learned helplessness and depression (Alloy, et al., 2009; Cole et al., 2007; Haine, Ayers, Sandler, Wolchik, & Weyer, 2003).

A related finding was that biological paternal figures play a significant role in parenting African-American men throughout their children's lifespans. Spreading awareness in this area would serve to strengthen African-American families, thus, lessening the potential of African-American males to suffer from attachment and depression problems in adulthood. Community mentor programs could be essential in spreading awareness to youth about the negative lifelong impact of paternal absence and potentially lessen the number of children being raised without biological paternal figures in the future.

Conclusions

The study findings indicated that there was a correlation between limited or no paternal presence during childhood and attachment difficulties and depression in adulthood. A 2x3 ANOVA found that attachment styles and paternal presence had a statistically significant interaction on depression propensities for the study's participants. Additionally, the main effects for attachment style and paternal presence revealed an effect that suggested that paternal absence during childhood could cause insecure attachment difficulties in adulthood. These results would indicate that there was a link between biological paternal absence and attachment difficulties in adulthood. An individual who suffers from attachment difficulties may experience problems maintaining healthy, long-term relationships in adulthood. These results aligned with scholarly findings that associated negative attachment experiences in childhood with an increase risk for developing depression later in life (Ainsworth, 2000; Alloy, Abramson, Grant, & Liu, 2009; Baldaro, 2010; Beck, 1967; Bowlby, 1980; Surcinelli, Rossi, & Montebarocci, 2010).

The founder of the attachment theory, John Bowlby (1963), pontificated that there was a direct relationship to an individual's childhood attachment experiences and depression propensities. He explained that weak childhood attachments is a direct precursor for one developing a negative self-image, that may cause them to feel unsupported, lonely, sad, and unlovable making one more susceptible to suffer from depression in adulthood. Aaron Beck (1967) agreed with this theory, concluding that negative thought patterns that are developed from a dysfunctional belief system, serve as the formation for depression. These historical theories along with this study's findings should serve to encourage awareness of the important role paternal figures play in childhood. The literature review found limited studies that focused on African-American men and whether there was a correlation between paternal absence, attachment style, and depression propensities. Because there is a high number of African-American children, reared with limited to no paternal presence in their life, it is hoped that this study will serve as a spring board for future research in this area.

References

Acock, A. C., & Kiecolt, K. J. (1989). Is it family structure or socioeconomic status? Family structure during adolescence and adult adjustment. *Social Forces, 68*, 553-571. doi: 10.1093/sf/68.2.553

Ainsworth, M. D. S. (1967). *Infancy in Uganda: Infant care and the growth of love.* Baltimore, MD: John Hopkins University Press

Ainsworth, M. D. S., Blehar, M. C., Walters, E., & Walls, S. (1978). *Patterns of attachment: A psychological study of the strange situation.* Hillsdale, NJ: Lawrence Erlbaum Associates

Ainsworth, P. (2000). *Understanding depression.* Jackson, MS: University Press of Mississippi

Allen, J. P., Hauser, S. T., Borman-Spurrell, E. (1996). Attachment theory as a framework for understanding sequelae of severe adolescent psychopathology: An 11-year-follow-up study. *Journal of Consulting and Clinical Psychology, 64*, 254-263. doi: 0022-006x/96

Alloy, L. B., Abramson, D. G., Grant, D., Liu, R. (2009). Vulnerability to unipolar depression: Cognitive-behavioral mechanisms. In K. Salzinger and M. R. Serper (Eds.), *Behavioral mechanisms and psychopathology: Advancing the explanation of its nature, cause, and treatment* (pp. 107-140). Washington, DC: American Psychological Association

Amato, P. R. (1991). Parental absence during childhood and depression in later life. *The Sociological Quarterly, 32*, 543-556

American Psychiatric Association (2000). *Diagnostic and statistical manual of mental disorders* (4th ed). Arlington, TX: American Psychiatric Association

Anderson, L. & Stevens, N. (1993). Associations between early experience with parents and well-being in old age. *Journal of Gerontology, 48*, 109-116

Battle, S. F. (2002). African American males at a crossroad. *Journal of Health and Social Policy, 15*, 81-91

Baxter, J. & Alexander, M. (2008). Mothers' work-to-family strain in single and couple parent families: the role of job characteristics and supports. *Australian Journal of Social Issues, 43*, 195-214

Beaty, L. A. (1995). Effects of paternal absence on male adolescents' peer relations and self-image. *Adolescence, 30*, 80

Beck, A. T., & Alford, B. A. (2009). *Depression: Causes and treatments* (2nd ed.). Philadelphia, PA: University of Pennsylvania Press

Beck, A.T., Rush, J.A., Shaw, B.F., & Emery, G. (1979). *Cognitive therapy of depression.* New York, NY: Guilford Press

Belsky, J. (1999). Modern evolutionary theory and patterns of attachment. In J. Cassidy and P.R. Shaver (Eds.), *Handbook of Attachment: Theory, Research, and Clinical Implications* (pp.141-161). New York, NY: Guilford Press

Benson, J. B., & Haith, M. M. (2009). *Social and emotional development in infancy and early childhood.* Oxford, UK: Elsevier

Berry, K., Barrowclough, C., & Wearden, A. (2009). Adult attachment, perceived earlier experiences of caregiving and trauma in people with psychosis. *Journal of mental Health, 18*, 280-287

Bettman, J. E. (2006). Using attachment theory to understand the treatment of depression. *Clinical Social Work Journal, 34*, 531-544. doi:10.1007/s10615-005-0033-1

Blau, D. M. (2008). A demographic analysis of the family structure experiences of children in the United States. *Review of Economics of the Household, 6*, 193-221. doi:10.1007/s11150-008-9030-9

Bowlby, J. (1980). *Loss, sadness and depression.* New York: Basic Books

Bowlby, J. (1982). *Attachment.* New York, NY: Basic Books

Bowlby, J. (1988). *A secure base: Parent-child attachment and healthy human development.* New York, NY: Basic Books

Bowlby, R. (2007). Babies and toddlers in non-parental day care can avoid stress and anxiety if they develop a lasting secondary attachment bond with one carer who is consistently accessible to them. *Attachment & Human Development, 9*, 307–319

Bowlby, J. (1973). *Separation: Anxiety and anger.* New York, NY: Basic Books

Brandimart, P. (2011). *Quantitative methods: An introduction for business management.* Hoboken, NJ: Wiley

Brown, L. (2007). Introducing the essence of parenting: A parenting program drawing on attachment. *Post-Script: Postgraduate Journal of Educational Research, 8*, 61-73

Bretheron, I. (1990). Communication patterns, internal working models and the intergenerational transmission of attachment relationships. *Infant Mental Health Journal, 11*, 237-252

Bretheron, I. (1995). A communication perspective on attachment relationships and internal working models. *Monographs of the Society for Research in Child Development, 60*, 310-329. doi:10.1111/1540-5834.ep9601091906

Bretherton, I. & Munholland, K. A. (1999). Internal working models in attachment relationships: A construct revisited. In J. Cassidy and P.R. Shaver (Eds.). *Handbook of Attachment: Theory, Research, and Clinical Implications* (pp. 89-111). New York, NY: Guilford Press

Brumariu, L. E. & Kerns, K. A. (2010). Parent-child attachment and internalizing symptoms and adolescence: A review of empirical findings and future directions. *Development and Psychopathology, 22*, 177-203 doi:10.1017/S0954579409990344

Carranza, L. V., Kilmann, P. R., & Vendemia, J. M. (2009). Links between Characteristics and Attachment variables for college students of parental divorce. *Adolescence, 44*, 253

Carver, C. S. (1997). Measure of attachment qualities (Self-report measure). Retrieved from http://www.psy.miami.edu/faculty/ccarver/CCscales.html

Chester, C., Jones, D. J., Zalot, A., & Sterrett, E. (2007). The psychosocial adjustment of African American youth from single mother homes: The relative contribution of parents and peers. *Journal of Clinical Child and Adolescent Psychology, 36*, 356-366

Chrisler, J. C., & McCreary, D. R. (2010). *Handbook of gender research in psychology*. New York, NY: Springer

Cicchetti, D., Toth, S.L, & Lynch, M. (1995). Bowlby's dream comes full circle: The application of attachment theory to risk and psychopathology. In T.H. Ollendick & R.J. Prinz (Eds.). *Advances in Clinical Child Psychology, 17*, 1-75. New York, NY: Plenum Press

Cole-Detke, H. & Kobak, R. (1996). Attachment processes in eating disorder and depression. *Journal of Consulting and Clinical Psychology, 64*, 282-290

Cole, D. A., Warren, D. E., Dallaire, D. H., Lagrange, B., Travis, R., & Ciesla, J. A., (2007). Early predictors of helpless thoughts and behaviors in children & developmental precursors to depressive cognitions. *Clinical Child Psychology and Psychiatry, 12*, 295-312. doi:10.1177/1359104507075936

Colin, V. L. (1996). *Human attachment.* Philadelphia, PA: Temple University Press

Covell, K., & Turnbull, W. (1982). The long-term effects of father absence in childhood on male university students' sex role identity and personal adjustment. *Journal of Genetic Psychology, 141*, 271

Cowan, P. A., Cohn, D. A., Cowan, C. P., & Pearson, J. L. (1996). Parents' attachment histories and children's externalizing and internalizing behaviors: Exploring family systems models of linkage. *Journal of Consulting and Clinical Psychology, 64*, 53-63

Cummings, E.M., & Cicchetti, D. (1990). Attachment, depression, and the transmission of depression. In M.T. Greenberg, D. Cicchetti, & E.M. Cummings (Eds.) *Attachment in the Preschool Years* (pp. 339-372). Chicago, IL: University of Chicago Press

Crowell, J. A., Fraley, R. C., & Shaver, P. R. (1999). Measurement of individual differences in adolescent and adult attachment. In J. Cassidy and P. R. Shaver (Eds.), *Handbook of Attachment: Theory, Research, and Clinical Implications* (pp. 434-496). New York, NY: Guilford Press

Crowell, J. & Waters, K. (2005). Attachment representations, secure-base behavior, and the evolution of adult relationships. In Grossmann, K. E., Grossmann, K., & Waters, E. (Eds.). (2005). *Attachment from Infancy to Adulthood: The Major Longitudinal Studies* (pp. 223-244). New York, NY: Guilford Press

Daniels, S. (1986). Relationship of employment status to mental health and family variables in Black men from single-parent families. *Journal of Applied Psychology, 71*, 0021-9010

de Haas, M.A., Bakermans-Kranenberg, M. J., & van IJzendoorn, M. II. (1994). The adult attachment interview and questionnaires for attachment style, temperament and memories of parental behavior. *Journal of Genetic Psychology, 155*, 471-486

de Vaus, D. (2002). Analyzing social science data. London: Sage Publications

Del Giudice, M. (2008). Sex-biased ratio of avoidant/ambivalent attachment in middle childhood. *The British Journal of Developmental Psychology, 26,* 369-379 doi:10.1348/0266151007X243289

Del Giudice, M. (2009). Sex, attachment, and the development of reproductive strategies. *Behavioral and Brain Sciences, 32,* 1-67. doi:10.1017/S0140525X09000016

Draper, P., & Harpending, H. (1982). Father-absence and reproductive strategy: An evolutionary perspective. *Journal of Anthropological Research, 38,* 255-273

Eisen, A. R., & Schaefer, C. E. (2005). *Separation anxiety in children and adolescents: An individualized approach to assessment and treatment.* New York, NY: Guilford Press

Erdfelder, E., Faul, F., & Buchner, A. (1996). Gpower: A general power analysis program. *Behavior Research Methods, Instruments, & Computers, 28,* 1-11

Faul, F., Erdfelder, E., Buchner, A., & Lang, A.-G. (2009). Statistical power analyses using G*Power 3.1: Tests for correlation and regression analyses. *Behavior Research Methods, 41,* 1149-1160

Feeney, J. A., Noller, P., & Hanrahan, M. (1994). Assessing adult attachment. In M. B. Sperling & W. H. Berman (Eds.), *Attachment in Adults* (pp. 128-154). New York, NY: Guilford Press

Federal Interagency Forum on Child and Family Statistics. (2012). America's children: Key national indicators of well-being. Retrieved from Childstats.gov/americaschildren/famsoc1.asp

Fonagy, P., Leigh, T., Steele, M., Steele, H., Kennedy, R., Mattoon, G. (1996). The relation of attachment status, psychiatric classification, and response to psychotherapy. *Journal of Consulting and Clinical Psychology, 64,* 22-31

Fraley, R.C. & Shaver, P.R. (2000). Adult romantic attachment: Theoretical developments, emerging controversies, and unanswered questions. *Review of General Psychology, 4,* 132-154

Fraley, R. C., Waller, N. G., & Brennan, K. A. (2000). An item response theory analysis of self-report measures of adult attachment. *Journal of Personality and Social Psychology,78,* 350-365

Franzese, Robert, J. & Kam, Cindy (2007). Modeling and interpreting interactive hypotheses in regression analysis. Michigan: University of Michigan Press

Freud, S. (1989). *Sigmund Freud: An outline of psycho-analysis.* (J. Strachey, Trans.) New York, NY: W.W. Norton & Company. (Original work published 1949)

Greenberg, M. T., Decline, M., Speltz, M. L., & Endriga, M. C. (1997). The role of attachment processes in externalizing psychopathology in young children. In L. Atkinson & K. J. Zucker (Eds.), *Attachment and Psychopathology* (pp. 196-222). New York, NY: Guilford Press

Griffith, B. A. (2004). The structure and development of internal working models: An integrated framework for understanding clients and promoting wellness. *Journal of Humanistic Counseling, Education and Development*, 43, 2

Grossmann, K. E., Grossmann, K., & Zimmermann, P. (1999). A wider view of attachment and exploration: Stability and change during the years of immaturity. In J. Cassidy and P. R. Shaver (Eds.), *Handbook of Attachment: Theory, Research, and Clinical Implications* (pp. 760-786). New York, NY: Guilford Press

Hall, T. (2007). *Journal of Psychology and Theology*, 35, 14-28

Hautamaki, A., Hautamaki, L., Neuvonen, L., & Maliniemi-Piispanen, S. (2010). Transmission of attachment across three generations: Continuity and reversal. *Clinical Child Psychology and Psychiatry*, 15, 347-355. doi:10.1177/1359104510365451

Hazan C. & Shaver P.R. (1987). Romantic love conceptualized as an attachment process. *Journal of Personality and Social Psychology*, 52, 511-24

Hazan, C., & Shaver, P.R. (1990). Love and work: An attachment theoretical perspective. *Journal of Personality and Social Psychology*, 59, 270-280

Hazan, C., & Shaver, P.R. (1994). Attachment as an organizational framework for research on close relationships. *Psychological Inquiry*, 5, 1-22

Herzog, J.M. (1995). Men in the psychoanalytic situation: Encountering father hunger. *Psychoanalysis & Psychotherapy*, 12, 46-59

Hesse, E. (1999). The adult attachment interview: Historical and current perspectives. In J. Cassidy and P.R. Shaver (Eds.), *Handbook of Attachment: Theory, Research, and Clinical Implications* (pp. 395-433). New York, NY: Guilford Press

Hinde, R. A., & Stevenson-Hinde, J. (1993). Perspectives on attachment. In Parkes, C. M., Stevenson-Hinde, J., & Marris,   P. (Eds.), *Attachment across the life cycle*, (pp. 52-63). New York, NY: Routledge

Hollist, D. R., & McBroom, W. H. (2006). Family structure, family tension, and self-reported marijuana use: A research finding of risky behavior among youths. *Journal of Sociology & Social Welfare*, 32, 283-292

Holmes, J. (1993). *John Bowlby and attachment theory*. New York, NY: Routledge

Horowitz, L. M., & Strack, S. (2011). *Handbook of interpersonal psychology: Theory, research, assessment and therapeutic interventions*. Hoboken, NJ: Wiley

Howe, D., Brandon, M., Hinings, D., & Schofield, G. (1999). *Attachment theory, child Maltreatment, and family support: A practice and assessment model*. Mahwah, NJ: Lawrence Erlbaum Associates

Iacoviello, B. M., Alloy, L. B., Abramson, L. Y., Choi, J. Y. (2010). The early course of depression: A longitudinal investigation of prodromal symptoms and their relation to symptomatic course of depressive episodes. *Journal of Abnormal Psychology*, 119, 459-467

Jaccard, J. & Becker, M. A., (2002). *Statistics for the behavioral sciences 4*. Belmont, CA: Wadsworth/Thomson Learning

Jagacinski, R. J., & Flach, J. M. (2003). *Control theory for humans: Quantitative approaches to modeling performance*. Mahwah, NJ: Lawrence Erlbaum Associates

Kagel, S. A., & Schilling, K. M. (1985). Sexual identification and gender identity among father-absent males. *Sex Roles*, 13, 357-370

Kalil, A., & Ryan, R. M. (2010). Mother's economic conditions and sources of support in fragile families. *Future of Children*, 20, 39-61

Kamkar, K., Doyle, A., & Markiewicz, D. (2012). Insecure attachment to parents and depressive symptoms in early adolescence: Mediating roles of attributions and self-esteem. *International Journal of Psychological Studies*, 4, 3-18. doi:10.5539/ijps.v4n2p3

Kenny, M. E. & Sirin, Selcuk, R. (2006). Parental attachment, self-worth and depressive symptoms among emerging adults. *Journal of Counseling and Development,* 84, 1-12

Kesner, J. E., & McKenry, P. C. (2001). Single parenthood and social competence in children of color. *Families in Society,* 82, 136-144

Kobak, R., Sudler, N. & Gamble, W. (1992). Attachment and depressive symptoms during adolescence: A developmental pathways analysis. *Development and Psychopathology,* 3, 461-474

Kogan, S. M., & Brody, G. H. (2010). Linking parenting and informal mentor processes to depressive symptoms among rural African American young adult men. *Cultural Diversity and Ethnic Minority Psychology,* 16, 299-306

Korkeila, J., Vahtera, J., Nabi, H., Kivimaki, M., Korkeila, K., Sumanen, M., Koskenvuo, K., & Koskenvuo, M., (2010). Childhood adversities, adulthood life events and depression. *Journal of Affective Disorders,* 127, 130-138, doi:10.1016/j.physletb.2003.10.071

Lee, E. J. (2003). *The attachment system throughout the life course: Review and criticisms of attachment theory.* Retrieved from http://www.personalityresearch.org/papers/lee.html(Erişim: 29/01/2012)

Liu, Y. (2006). Paternal/maternal attachment, peer support social expectations of peer interaction, and depressive symptoms. *Adolescence,* 41.705

Lyons-Ruth, K. & Block, D. (1996). The disturbed caregiving system: Relations among childhood trauma, maternal caregiving, and infant effect and attachment. *Infant Mental Health Journal,* 17, 257-275

Lyons-Ruth, K. (2006). The interface between attachment and intersubjectivity: perspective from the longitudinal study of disorganized attachment

Mackey, W. C. (1998). Father presence: An enhancement of a child's well-being. *The Journal of Men's Studies,* 6, 227-236

Marczyk, G. R., DeMatteo, D., &Festinger, D. (2005).*Essentials of research design and methodology.* Hoboken, NJ: Wiley

Maier, E. H. & Lachman, M. E. (2000). Consequences of early parental loss and separation for health and well-being in midlife. *International Journal of Behavioral Development,* 24, 183-189

Main, M. (1996). Introduction for the special edition on attachment and psychopathology: Overview of the field of attachment. *Journal of Consulting and Clinical Psychology, 64,* 237-243

McDonald, J. D., (2008). Measuring personality constructs: The advantages and disadvantages of self-reports, informant reports and behavioural assessments. *Enquire, 1,* 1-19. McDowell, D.J., & Parke, R.D. (2009). Parental correlates of children's peer relations: An empirical test of a tripartite model. In Bachmann, R. & Zaheer, A. (Eds.), *Handbook on trust research* (pp. 29-52). North Hampton, MA: Edward Elgar 123 Publishing, Inc.

Mercer, J. (2006). *Understanding attachment: Parenting, child care and emotional development.* Praeger: Westport: CT

Mikulincer, M., Shaver, P. R., Sapir-Lavid, Y., & Avihou-Kanza, N. (2009). What's script and its associations with attachment-style dimensions. *Journal of Personality and Social Psychology, 97,* 615-633. doi:10.1037/a0015649

Mitchell, M. & Jolley, J. (2004). *Research and Design Explained.* Belmont, CA: Wadsworth/Thomas Learning

Mowder, B. A., Rubinson, F., & Yasik, A. E. (2009). *Evidence-based practice in infant and early childhood psychology.* Hoboken, NJ: Wiley

National Institute of Mental Health (2005). Depression and men. Retrieved from http://www.nimh.nih.gov/health/publications/men-and depression/men- and-depression.PDF

Nelson, J.K., & Bennett, C.S. (2008). Introduction: Special issue on attachment. *Clinical Social Work Journal, 36,* 3-7. doi: 10.1007/s10615-007-0114-4

Newland, L. A., & Coyl, D. D. (2010). Fathers' role as attachment figures: An interview with Sir Richard Bowlby. *Early Child Development & Care, 180,* 25-32. doi:10.1080/03004430903414679

Nicolosi, J. (1991). *Reparative counseling of male homosexuality: A new clinical approach.* Northvale, NJ: Jason Aronson

Oliver, L. E. (2003). Perceptions of parents and partners and men's depressive symptoms. *Journal of Social and Personal Relationships, 20,* 621-635. doi:01177/02654075030205003

Paschall, M.J., Ringwalt, C., & Flewelling, R.L. (2003). Effects of parenting, father absence, and affiliation with delinquent peers on delinquent behavior among African-American male adolescents. *Adolescence, 38,* 15

Peluso, P. R., Peluso, J. P., White, A. F., & Kern, R. M. (2004). A comparison of attachment: A review of the literature. *Journal of Counseling & Development, 82,* 139

Pollock, J. M., Mullings, J. L., Crouch, B. M. (2006). Violent women: Findings from the Texas women inmates study. *Journal of Interpersonal Violence, 21,* 485-502. doi: 10.1177/0886260505285722

Popenoe, D. (1997). Life without a father. Paper presented at the Annual Conference of the NCFR Fatherhood and Motherhood in a Diverse and Changing World, Arlington, VA

Priel, B. & Shamai, D. (1995). Attachment style and perceived social support: Effects on affect regulation. *Personality and Individual Differences, 19,* 235-241

Prior, V., Glaser, D., & Kingsley, J. (2006). *Understanding Attachment and Attachment Disorders: Theory, Evidence, and Practice*. Philadelphia, PA: Jessica Kingsley

Rholes, W.S. & Simpson, J.A. (2004). Attachment theory: Basic concepts and contemporary questions. In W.S. Rholes and J.A. Simpson (Eds.), *Adult Attachment: Theory, Research, and Clinical Implications*, pp. 3–14. New York, NY: Guilford Press

Roberts, J.E., Gotlib, I.H., & Kassel, J.D. (1996). Adult attachment security symptoms of depression: The mediating roles of dysfunctional attitudes and low self-esteem. *Journal of Personality and Social Psychology, 70,* 310-320

Rosenstein, D. S. & Horowitz, H. A. (1996). Adolescent attachment and psychopathology. *Journal of Consulting and Clinical Psychology, 64,* 244-253

Ross, L. R., McKim, M. K., & Ditommaso, E. (2006). How do underlying "self" and "other" dimensions define adult attachment styles? *Canadian Journal of Behavioural Science, 38,* 294

Ruijten, T., Roelofs, J., & Rood, L. (2011). The mediating role of rumination in the relation between quality of attachment relations and depressive symptoms in non-clinical adolescents. *Journal of Child & Family Studies, 20,* 452-459. doi:10.1007/s10825-01009412-5

Seutter, R.A., & Rovers, M. (2004). Emotionally absent fathers: Furthering the understanding of homosexuality. *Journal of Psychology and Theology, 32*(1), 43-49. doi: 0091-6471/410-730

Seligman, M. E. P. (1975). *Helplessness: On depression, development and death.* San Francisco, CA: W. H. Freeman

Schmider, E., Ziegler, M., Danay, E., Beyer, L., Buhner, M., (2010). Is it really robust?: Reinvestigating the robustness of ANOVA against violations of the normal distribution assumption. *Methodology: European Journal of Research Methods for the Behavioral and Social Sciences*, 147-151. doi:10.1027/1614-2241/a000016

Schur, M. (1960). Discussion of Dr. John Bowlby's paper. *Psychoanalytical Study of the Child*, 15, 63-84

Shah, P.E., Fonagy, P., & Stratheam, L. (2010). Is attachment transmitted across generations? The plot thickens. *Clinical Child Psychology and Psychiatry*, 15, 329-346. doi: 10.117/1359104510365449

Shao, J. (1999). *Mathmatical statistics.* Secaucus, NJ: Springer

Sherry, A., Lyddon, W. J. Henson, R. K. (2007). Adult attachment and developmental personality styles: An empirical study. *Journal of Counseling and Development*, 85, 337-348

Simpson, J. A. (1999). Attachment theory in evolutionary perspective. In J. Cassidy & P. R. Shaver (Eds.). *Handbook of attachment: Theory, research, and clinical applications* (pp. 115-140). New York: NY: Guilford Press

Sloman, L., Price, J., Gilbert, P., & Gardner, R. (1994). Adaptive function of depression: Psychotherapeutic implications. *American Journal of* Psychotherapy, 48

Sobolewski, J. M., & Amato, P. R. (2005). Economic hardship in the family of origin and children's psychological well-being in adulthood. *Journal of Marriage and Family*, 67(1)

Sroufe, L. A. & Waters, E. (1977). Attachment as an organizational construct. Retrieved from http://psychology.psy.sunysb.edu/ewaters/552/PDF_Files/OrgConstruct.PDF

Surcinelli, P., Rossi, N. Montebarocci, O., & Baldaro, B. (2010). *Adult attachment styles and psychological disease: Examining the mediating role of personality traits.* Country Publication, 144, 523-534

Target, M., & Gerber, A. (1996). The relation of attachment status, psychiatric classification, and response to psychotherapy. *Journal of Consulting and Clinical Psychology*, 64 (1), 22-31

Tavakol, M. & Dennick, R. (2011). Making sense of cronbach's alpha. *International Journal of Medical Education*, 253-255. doi: 10.5116/ijme.4dfb.8dfd

United States Department of Labor Bureau of Labor Statistics (2013). National Longitudinal Survey. Retrieved from http://www.bls.gov/nls/nlsy97.htm

van IJzendoorn, M. H. & Bakermans-Kranenburg, M. J. (1996). Attachment representations in mothers, fathers, adolescents, and clinical groups: A meta-analytic search for normative data. *Journal of Consulting and Clinical Psychology*, 64 (1), 8-21

van IJzendoorn, M.H. & Bakermans-Kranenburg, M.J. (2009). Erratum/corrigendum no reliable gender differences in attachment across the lifespan. *Behavorial and Brain Sciences*, 32, 247-248. doi: 10.1017/S0140525X09000843

van IJzendoorn, M. H. & Bakermans-Kranenburg, M. J. (2010). Invariance of adult attachment across gender, age, culture, and socioeconomic status? *Journal of Social and Personal Relationships*, 27, 200-208. doi:10.1177/0265407509360908

Weathington, B. L., Cunningham, C. J., & Pittenger, D. J. (2010). *Research methods for the behavioral and social sciences*. Hoboken, NJ: Wiley

Wauterickx, N., Gouwy, A., & Bracke, P. (2006). Parental divorce and depression: Long-term effects on adult children. *Journal of Divorce & Remarriage*, 45(3), 43-60. doi: 10.1300/J087v45n03_03

Weinfield, N. S., Sroufe, L. A., Egeland, B., & Carlson, E. A. (1999). The Nature of individual differences in infant-caregiver attachment. In J. Cassidy and P.R. Shaver (Eds.), *Handbook of Attachment: Theory, Research, and Clinical Implications* (pp. 68-88). New York, NY: Guilford Press

Wildeman, C. (2009). Parental imprisonment, the prison boom, and the concentration of childhood disadvantage. *Demography*, 46, 265-280

Wildeman, C & Western, B. (2010). Incarceration in fragile families. *Future of Children*, 20, 157-177

Wright, G. & Czelusta, J. (2007). Resource-based growth past and present. In D. Lederman & W. Maloney (Eds.). *Natural Resources: Neither Curse Nor Destiny*

Zhan, M. (2006). Economic mobility of single mothers: The role of assets and human capital development. *Journal of Sociology and Social Welfare*, 33, 127

Zepf, S., Zepf, J. A., & Turnbull (2006). Attachment theory and psychoanalysis: Some remarks from an epistemological and from a Freudian viewpoint. *International Journal of Psychoanalysis*, 87, 1529-1548

APPENDIX A

Dear Research Participant:

I would like to take the time out to thank you for your participation in my research study. It is important for you to understand that your participation in this research is strictly voluntary and you will not be penalized at any time if you decide that you do not want to participate.

Enclosed in this research packet, you will find an informed consent form and three surveys. If you have any questions while completing these forms, please raise your hand and I will come to you. After you have signed and dated the inform consent form and completed the surveys, please fold the research packet and place it in the designated lock box, which will be located by the door. Please keep this letter in your possession to assist you with any future questions.

In order to ensure that your information remains confidential, besides your printed signature and name on the informed consent form, please do not provide your name, initials, address, phone number, or any other identifying information on any of the forms.

If you have any questions or concerns after completing the research packet, you can contact me directly.

Your participation in this research is greatly appreciated.

Michelle Tyrus, MA
Doctoral Candidate

APPENDIX B

CONSENT FORM
You are invited to participate in a research study that sets out to examine the possible impact that being reared in a mother headed, single-parent household without the biological father has on attachment and depression propensities for adult African-American men. You have been selected to participate in this study because it was designed for African-American men between the ages 18 to 55, who have been raised in a mother headed, single-parent home without a biological father.

This form is part of a process called "informed consent" that will assist you in understanding this study prior to making a decision whether to participate.

This study is being conducted by Michelle Tyrus, a doctoral psychology student attending Walden University.

Background Information:
The purpose of this study is to examine whether African-American men who were reared in a home without their biological father have a high propensity to suffer from attachment and depression in adulthood.

Procedures:
If you agree to participate in this study, you will be asked to do the following:

- Read this consent form carefully and if you have any questions please ask me.

- Be sure to **not place your name on any of the forms that will be provided to you.**

- Voluntarily complete 3 surveys, which will take approximately 30 minutes to complete.

- Voluntarily fold your completed surveys and return it to me. If you choose, you can mail the surveys to me in a self-addressed, stamped, envelope that will be provided at your request by me.

Voluntary Nature of the Study:
Your participation in this study is completely voluntary, which means that everyone will respect your decision of whether or not you want to participate in the study.

Additionally, if you decide to join the study now, you can still change your mind during the study. If you feel anxious or stressed during the study, you may stop at any time. It is also within your rights to pass any questions that you feel are too personal.

Risks and Benefits of Being in the Study:
There are some risks associated with this study, as the participant may feel stress or depressed after completing the surveys. A therapist referral list will be included in the research packet for

your convenience, if at any time you feel the need to talk with someone after filling out the surveys.

The benefit of your taking part in this study is that the information gathered will assist in the investigation of whether depression symptoms are influenced by the absence of paternal presence. This study may provide evidence that African-American men may benefit from having consistent male role models.

Compensation:
Your voluntary participation in this study indicates that you have full knowledge that there will be no compensation or incentives for your participation in this research.

Confidentiality:
All information you provide will be kept anonymous. This researcher will not use any demographic information provided by you for any purposes outside of the scope of this research.

Contacts and Questions:
You may ask this researcher any questions at the time you have been provided this consent packet; if you have any questions later, you may contact me via telephone at (720) 296-8613 and/or via email at michelletyrus@yahoo.com. You may keep the consent form for your records. If you want to talk privately about your rights as a participant, you can contact Dr. Leilani Endicott. She is the Walden University representative who can discuss this with you. Walden University's approval number for this study is 08-26-13-0101984 and it expires on August 25, 2014.

Statement of Consent:
I have read the above information and I feel I understand the study well enough to make a decision about my involvement. I also understand by completing the attached surveys and returning them to me, I am agreeing to all the terms that have been described above.

APPENDIX C

IN ORDER TO PROTECT YOUR PRIVACY, PLEASE DO NOT PUT YOUR NAME ON THIS FORM.

PLEASE ANSWER THE FOLLOWING QUESTIONS. THIS INFORMATION WILL BE USED SOLELY FOR THE PURPOSE OF INFORMATION COLLECTION AND WILL NOT BE USED IN ANY WAY TO IDENTIFY YOU. IF YOU HAVE ANY QUESTIONS, PLEASE FEEL FREE TO ASK.

1. Age:

☐ 18-23
☐ 24-29
☐ 30-35
☐ 36-41
☐ 42-47
☐ 48-55

2. Highest Educational Level:

☐ Didn't Complete High School
☐ GED
☐ High School Graduate
☐ Associate's Degree
☐ Bachelor's Degree
☐ Master's Degree
☐ Doctorate

3. Marital Status:

☐ Single
☐ Married
☐ Widowed
☐ Separated
☐ Divorced

4. Number of times married:

☐ 0
☐ 1
☐ 2
☐ 3+

5. Up to age of 13 years, how many years were you in the home with your biological father?

☐ Less than 1 year
☐ 1-6 years
☐ 7-12 years

6. How often during childhood did you experience sadness?

☐ 0 years
☐ 1-6 years
☐ 7-12 years
☐ 13-18 years

7. During adulthood how often do you experience feelings of sadness?

☐ 0 years
☐ 1-6 years
☐ 7-12 years
☐ 13-18 years
☐ 19+ years

APPENDIX D

Copyright Permission for MAQ

I apologize for this automated reply. All measures I have developed are available for research and teaching applications without charge and without need to request permission; we ask only that you cite their source in any report that results. If you wish to use a measure for a purpose other than that, you must also contact the copyright holder, the publisher of the journal in which the measure was published.

Information concerning the measure you are asking about can be found at the website below. I think most of your questions will be answered there. If questions remain, however, do not hesitate to contact me. Good luck in your work.

http://www.psy.miami.edu/faculty/ccarver/CCscales.html

APPENDIX E

Measures of Attachment Qualities (MAQ)

IN ORDER TO PROTECT YOUR PRIVACY, PLEASE DO NOT PUT YOUR NAME ON THIS FORM.
Respond to each of the following statements by expressing how much you agree with it (if you do generally agree) or how much you disagree with it (if you generally disagree). Make all your responses on the answer sheet only. Do not leave any items blank. Please be as accurate as you can be throughout, and try especially hard not to let your answer to any one item influence your answer to any other item. Treat each one as though it is completely unrelated to the others. There are no right or wrong answers, you are simply to express your own personal feelings and opinions. Choose from these reponse options:

1 = I DISagree with the statement a lot
2 = I DISagree with the statement a little
3 = I agree with the statement a little
4 = I agree with the statement a lot

1. When I'm close to someone, it gives me
   a sense of comfort about life in general.   1 2 3 4

2. I often worry that my partner doesn't really love me.   1 2 3 4

3. I have trouble getting others to be as close
   as I want them to be.   1 2 3 4

4. I find it easy to get close to others.   1 2 3 4

5. I often worry my partner will not want to stay with me.   1 2 3 4

6. Others want me to be more intimate than
   I feel comfortable being.   1 2 3 4

7. It feels relaxing and good to be close to someone.   1 2 3 4

8. I am very comfortable being close to others.   1 2 3 4

9. I don't worry about others abandoning me.   1 2 3 4

10. My desire to merge sometimes scares people away.   1 2 3 4

11. I prefer not to be too close to others.   1 2 3 4

12. I find others are reluctant to get as close as I would like.   1 2 3 4

13. I get uncomfortable when someone wants to be very close.   1 2 3 4

14. Being close to someone gives me a source of
    strength for other activities.   1 2 3 4

THANK YOU FOR YOUR PARTICIPATION

APPENDIX F

CURRICULUM VITAE

ACADEMIC EXPERIENCE

2005 to Present   Candidate for Doctorate of Philosophy – Clinical Psychology, Walden University, Minneapolis, MN

                         Anticipated Graduation Date March 2014

2003 to 2004   Masters of Arts in Organizational Management
University of Phoenix, Denver, CO

1991 to 1996   Bachelor's of Science in Sociology
Kansas State University, Manhattan, KS

RELEVANT PROFESSIONAL EXPERIENCE

2011 to Present   **Psychological Test Examiner / Doctoral Candidate**
Third Way Youth Center

Duties: Interview and counsel youth who reside at the center. Administer a battery of assessments depending on the needs of the client and generate psychological evaluations.

2010 to 2011   **Doctoral Psychology Intern**
Third Way Youth Center
Duties: Provide inpatient mental health services (individual, group, and family therapy) to youth who reside at the facility. Design treatment plans, diagnose clients, consult with Juvenile Justice Department, conduct psychological assessments and generate psychological evaluations.

2009 to 2010   **Doctoral Practicum Intern**
Nicoletti-Flater & Associates

Duties: Provide mental health services (individual and family therapy). Design treatment plans and write psychological evaluations. Conduct risk assessments for clients and interview clients.

HONORS AND REWARDS

2005   inducted as a lifetime member of Psi Chi Honor Society

PROFESSIONAL MEMBERSHIPS

2006   American Psychological Association (APA)
              Student Member

2012   The Association of Black Psychologists (ABPsi)
              Student Member